The Genius
of American Politics

The Genius
of American Politics

By

DANIEL J. BOORSTIN

THE UNIVERSITY OF CHICAGO PRESS

CHICAGO AND LONDON

THE UNIVERSITY OF CHICAGO PRESS, CHICAGO, 60637
The University of Chicago Press, Ltd., London W. C. 1

FOR

PAUL, JONATHAN, AND DAVID

"... *like Genius, simple: that is why
they are the immortal teachers.*"

AUTHOR'S NOTE

THIS volume is a revision of public lectures delivered at the University of Chicago in February and March 1952, under the Charles R. Walgreen Foundation for the Study of American Institutions. Professor Jerome G. Kerwin, director of the Foundation, has been especially helpful with his encouragement and criticism. Some of the materials of the lectures were developed in connection with my teaching at the University of Rome under a Fulbright appointment in 1950–51. Parts of chapter iii appeared in the *William and Mary Quarterly* for October, 1950. A grant from the Social Science Research Committee of the University of Chicago has aided the preparation of the manuscript. I particularly wish to thank William T. Bluhm, now of the department of political science of the University of Rochester, for his trenchant editorial advice. To the many friends who have read the manuscript and offered their suggestions I am deeply in debt. Without the stimulus of my wife, Ruth F. Boorstin, this volume could hardly have come into being: she has been the principal editor of the manuscript.

ACKNOWLEDGMENTS

I WISH to thank the following publishers for permission to quote from copyright books or periodicals bearing their imprint: Columbia University Press (Louis M. Hacker, *The Triumph of American Capitalism*); Harvard University Press (Josiah Royce, *Fugitive Essays*); Henry Holt and Company (Frederick Jackson Turner, *The Frontier in American History*); Alfred A. Knopf, Inc. (James Stevens, *Paul Bunyan;* and Alexis de Tocqueville, ed. Phillips Bradley, *Democracy in America*); Lincoln-Mercury Times (Aldous Huxley, "A Tour through Time"); Longmans, Green and Company (William James, *Varieties of Religious Experience*); National Bibliophile Service (Carl Becker, *The Declaration of Independence*); Oxford University Press (Samuel Eliot Morison and Henry Steele Commager, *The Growth of the American Republic*); Rinehart and Company (Stephen Vincent Benét, *John Brown's Body*); Yale University Press (Carl Becker, *The Heavenly City of the Eighteenth Century Philosophers*, and John Dewey, *A Common Faith*).

TABLE OF CONTENTS

"*Pompey then penetrated into the Sanctuary, in order to satisfy his curiosity as to the nature of the Judaean worship, about which the most contradictory reports prevailed. The Roman general was not a little astonished at finding within the sacred recesses of the Holy of Holies, neither an ass's head nor, indeed, images of any sort.*"

GRAETZ, *History of the Jews*, II, 66.

"*When the temple was occupied by successive conquerors, Pompey the Great and . . . Titus Caesar, they found there nothing of the kind, but the purest type of religion, the secrets of which we may not reveal to aliens.*"

JOSEPHUS *Against Apion* ii. 82.

INTRODUCTION

THE genius of American democracy comes not from any special virtue of the American people but from the unprecedented opportunities of this continent and from a peculiar and unrepeatable combination of historical circumstances. These circumstances have given our institutions their character and their virtues. The very same facts which explain these virtues, explain also our inability to make a "philosophy" of them. They explain our lack of interest in political theory, and why we are doomed to failure in any attempt to sum up our way of life in slogans and dogmas. They explain, therefore, why we have nothing in the line of a theory that can be exported to other peoples of the world.

The thesis of this book is that nothing could be more un-American than to urge other countries to imitate America. We should not ask them to adopt our "philosophy" because we have no philosophy which can be exported. My argument is simple. It is based on forgotten commonplaces of American history—facts so obvious that we no longer see them. I argue, in a word, that American democracy is unique. It possesses a "genius" all its own. By this I mean what the Romans might have described as the tutelary spirit assigned to our nation at its birth and presiding over its destiny. Or what we more prosaically might call a characteristic disposition of our culture.

In one sense, of course, everybody has a political theory, even if it is expressed only in hostility to theories. But this is a barren paradox, concealing more than it discovers. In our political life we have been like Molière's M. Jourdain, who was astonished to discover that all his life he had been speaking prose. We have not been much interested in the grammar of politics. We have been more interested in the way it works than in the theory behind it. Our unique history has thus offered us those benefits which come (in Edmund Burke's words) "from considering our liberties in the light of an inheritance" and has led us away from "extravagant and presumptuous speculations."

The great political theorists—men like Plato, Aristotle, Augustine, Hobbes, Locke, and Rousseau—even when not guilty of "extravagant and presumptuous speculations," have been primarily interested in discovering and systematizing general truths about society, regardless of time and place. However much they may have differed in other matters, they have all had in common an attempt to *abstract*, to separate the universal principles of all societies and governments from the peculiar circumstances of their own society and government. Much of what we understand comes from the light which they have thrown, from their different vantage points, on the problem of government. The United States has never produced a political philosopher of their stature or a systematic theoretical work to rank with theirs.

But I mean something more when in this book I speak of our antipathy to political theory. Especially in our own age (and at least since the French Revolution of

Introduction

1789), more and more of the world has sought in social theory no mere rationale for institutions but a blueprint for remaking society. Rousseau and Marx, for example, have been put to this use. Recent European politics shows us men of all complexions seeking an explicit orthodoxy for society. Burke was one of the first to note this tendency and its dangers, when he observed, "The bulk of mankind on their part are not excessively curious concerning any theories, whilst they are really happy; and one sure symptom of an ill-conducted state is the propensity of the people to resort to them." A pretty good rule-of-thumb for us in the United States is that our national well-being is in inverse proportion to the sharpness and extent of the theoretical differences between our political parties.

The tendency to abstract the principles of political life may sharpen issues for the political philosopher. It becomes idolatry when it provides statesmen or a people with a blueprint for their society. The characteristic tyrannies of our age—naziism, fascism, and communism—have expressed precisely this idolatry. They justify their outrages because their "philosophies" require them.

One of the many good fortunes of American civilization has been the happy coincidence of circumstances which has led us away from such idolatry. It is my belief that the circumstances which have stunted our interest in political philosophy have also nourished our refusal to make our society into the graven image of any man's political philosophy. In other ages this refusal might have

3

seemed less significant; in ours it is a hallmark of a decent, free, and God-fearing society.

If what I say is true, it has profound consequences both for our understanding of ourselves and for our relation to Europe. It speaks to those who say that what we need in this country is a clearer "philosophy" of democracy. It speaks to those who think we should try to compete with the Russians in a war of philosophies. This book adds up to a warning that, if we rely on the "philosophy of American democracy" as a weapon in the world-wide struggle, we are relying on a weapon which may prove a dud. It may prove so because, as I shall try to show in this book, the peculiar strengths of American life have saved us from the European preoccupation with political dogmas and have left us inept and uninterested in political theory.

Anyone who has recently been abroad and heard the sort of thing we are telling the world can say that it does not sound very good. The portraits of American life are sometimes admirable—of the public library, the general store, and the volunteer fire department. But the statements of what America believes (and therefore what Europe would be better by believing) make the American abroad uncomfortable, if not downright embarrassed. They say something which is not American at all, even if they are sometimes expressed with the engaging brashness of a Fourth of July oration. What is the matter with these general statements is not any weakness in our institutions or any special stupidity in our publicity writers. Actually, they are bad because of the peculiarities—and

4

even the advantages—of our geography, our history, and our way of life.

To understand the uniqueness of American history is to begin to understand why no adequate theory of our political life can be written. It will also help us to see why our institutions cannot be transplanted to other parts of the world. In the present world struggle, therefore, we should not hope to convert peoples to an American theory of government or expect to save western Europe from communism by transplanting American institutions. I want to develop this thesis not by discussing the rest of the world but by underlining a few facts of American history.

Although I shall set out from some of the most familiar facts of our past, in the course of this argument I shall lead you to some unfamiliar—and even paradoxical—conclusions about our political life. To understand these conclusions, you will need to reject some of the most widely accepted clichés about us. These clichés have been manufactured by our European friends and enemies. They go back to propaganda about us several centuries old, the labels made by the age of George III and earlier, which have stuck with amazing effectiveness.

From the earliest days, romantic Europeans have touted America as the country of novelty, of the unexpected and the untried, of grand visions and aspirations, where man could try out his latest inventions and test all those vagaries which were impossible in a conservative Europe. At the same time, conservative Europeans have attacked us for these very same dispositions, which to them, of course, have seemed vices. For many decades we were the Utopia of radicals and the Babel of conservatives. We have been given a reputation for being a country without tradition, without wholesome continuity in institutions, where *anything* might happen. This is what Europeans have agreed on, and their unanimity has forced our not always grudging assent. Now it is my thesis that, whatever may have been our weaknesses, this is not one of them.

I shall try to show how American history has nourished in a very special way and to an extraordinary degree our feeling for that principle of social science which I shall later call the "seamlessness" of culture. It is enough for the present to say that all this denies the stock European picture of us. Our geography and history have led us to an unspoken assumption, an axiom, so basic to our thinking that we have hardly been aware of it at all. This is the axiom that institutions are not and should not be the grand creations of men toward large ends and outspoken values; rather they are organisms which grow out of the soil in which they are rooted and out of the tradition from which they have sprung. Our history has fitted us, even against our will, to understand the meaning of conservatism. We have become the exemplars of the continuity of history and of the fruits which come from cultivating institutions suited to a time and place, in continuity with the past.

This point, if it is true, has special importance today. For the first time in modern history, and to an extent not true even in the age of the French Revolution, Europe has become the noisy champion of man's power to make over his culture at will. Communism is, in one sense, the extravagances of the French Revolution rewritten on the Gargantuan scale and acting with the terrifying efficiency of the twentieth century. People all over Europe have been accustomed, since the eighteenth century, to the notion that man can better his condition by trying to remake his institutions in some colossal image. Fascism and naziism proposed this; and so does communism. Europe has not yet realized that the remedy it seeks is itself a disease.

In this book I shall be describing some of those peculiarities of our history which in the past have helped save us from the romantic illusion. We cannot properly understand them without defining clearly our own picture of our political character. In my first chapter I will describe some of the most general characteristics of American political thought. Chapters ii, iii, and iv will deal, in turn, with three great crises: the Puritan struggle against the wilderness, the American Revolution, and the Civil War. In each case I shall try to discover the effect of the event on our traditional attitude toward political theory, at the same time seeing how each crisis illustrates characteristics which run through all our history. Then, in chapter v, I shall turn to the special relation between religion and political thought in the United States and the peculiar significance of our talkativeness about our ideals. In my last chapter I shall try to draw together the threads, to see what, if anything, can be generalized about our political theory. Is there perhaps a theory behind our theory, or behind our lack of a theory, which might itself have some validity as a conscious principle of political thought?

I

HOW BELIEF IN THE EXISTENCE OF AN
AMERICAN THEORY HAS MADE
A THEORY SUPERFLUOUS

THE American must go outside his country and hear the voice of America to realize that his is one of the most spectacularly lopsided cultures in all history. The marvelous success and vitality of our institutions is equaled by the amazing poverty and inarticulateness of our theorizing about politics. No nation has ever believed more firmly that its political life was based on a perfect theory. And yet no nation has ever been less interested in political philosophy or produced less in the way of theory. If we can explain this paradox, we shall have a key to much that is characteristic—and much that is good —in our institutions.

In this chapter I shall attempt an explanation. I start from the notion that the two sides of the paradox explain each other. The very same facts which account for our belief that we actually possess a theory also explain why we have had little interest in political theories and have never bothered seriously to develop them.

For the belief that an explicit political theory is superfluous precisely because we already somehow possess a satisfactory equivalent, I propose the name "givenness."

"Givenness" is the belief that values in America are in some way or other automatically defined: *given* by certain facts of geography or history peculiar to us. The notion, as I shall outline it in the present chapter, has three faces, which I shall describe in turn. First is the notion that we have received our values as a gift from the *past;* that the earliest settlers or Founding Fathers equipped our nation at its birth with a perfect and complete political theory, adequate to all our future needs.

The second is the notion that in America we receive values as a gift from the *present*, that our theory is always implicit in our institutions. This is the idea that the "American Way of Life" harbors an "American Way of Thought" which can do us for a political theory, even if we never make it explicit or never are in a position to confront ourselves with it. It is the notion that to Americans political theory never appears in its nakedness but always clothed in the peculiar American experience. We like to think that, from the shape of the living experience, we can guess what lies underneath and that such a guess is good enough—perhaps actually better than any naked theory. While according to the first axiom of "givenness" our values are the gift of our history, according to the second they are the gift of our landscape.

The third part of "givenness" is a belief which links these two axioms. It is a belief in the *continuity* or homogeneity of our history. It is the quality of our experience which makes us see our national past as an uninterrupted continuum of similar events, so that our past merges indistinguishably into our present. This sense of continuity is what makes it easy for us to accept the two first axioms at the same time: the idea of a preformed original theory given to us by the Founding Fathers, and the idea of an impicit theory always offered us by our present experience. Our feeling of continuity in our history makes it easy for us to see the Founding Fathers as our contemporaries. It induces us to draw heavily on the materials of our history, but always in a distinctly nonhistorical frame of mind.

I. VALUES GIVEN BY THE PAST: THE
PREFORMATION IDEAL

Now I shall begin by trying to explain what I have called the first axiom of "givenness": the idea that values are a gift from our past. Here we face our conscious attitude toward our past and toward our way of inheriting from it. This particular aspect of the "givenness" idea may be likened to the obsolete biological notion of "preformation." That is the idea that all parts of an organism pre-exist in perfect miniature in the seed. Biologists used to believe that if you could look at the seed of an apple under a strong enough microscope you would see in it a minute apple tree. Similarly, we seem still to believe that if we could understand the ideas of the earliest settlers—the Pilgrim Fathers or Founding Fathers—we would find in them no mere seventeenth- or eighteenth-century philosophy of government but the perfect embryo of the theory by which we now live. We believe, then, that the mature political ideals of the nation existed clearly conceived in the minds of our patriarchs. The notion is essentially static. It assumes that the values and theory of the nation were given once and for all in the very beginning.

What circumstances of American history have made such a view possible? The first is the obvious fact that, unlike western European countries, where the coming of the first white man is shrouded in prehistoric mist, civilization in the United States stems from people who came to the American continent at a definite period in recent history. For American political thought this fact has had the greatest significance. We have not found it necessary to invent an Aeneas, for we have had our William Bradford and John Winthrop, or, looking to a later period, our Benjamin Franklin and James Madison. We have needed no Virgil to make a myth of the first settlement of our land or the first founding of the Republic; the crude facts of history have been good enough.

The facts of our history have thus made it easy for us to assume that our national life, as distinguished from that of the European peoples who trace their identity to a remote era, has had a clear purpose. Life in America—appropriately called "The American Experiment"—has again and again been described as the test or the proof of values supposed to have been clearly in the minds of the Founders. While, as we shall see, the temper of much of our thought has been antihistorical, it is nevertheless true that we have leaned heavily on history to clarify our image of ourselves. Perhaps never before, except conceivably in the modern state of Israel, has a nation so firmly believed that it was founded on a full-blown theory and hence that it might understand itself by recapturing a particular period in its past.

This idea is actually so familiar, so deeply imbedded in our thinking, that we have never quite recognized it as a characteristic, much less a peculiarity, of our political thought. Nor have we become aware of its implications. "Four score and seven years ago," Lincoln said at Gettysburg in 1863, "our fathers brought forth on this continent, *a new nation, conceived in Liberty, and dedicated to the proposition that all men are created equal.*" We have forgotten that these words are less the statement of a political theory than an affirmation that an adequate theory already existed at the first epoch of national life. As we shall see in a later chapter, this belief itself helps account for the way in which the traditional, conservative, and inarticulate elements of our Revolution have been forgotten. A few slogans have been eagerly grasped as if they gave the essence of our history. While the conservative and legal aspect of our Revolution has remained hidden from popular view, schoolboys and popular orators (who seldom read beyond the preambles of legal documents) have conceived the Declaration of Independence as written primarily, if not exclusively, to vindicate man's equality and his "inalienable rights to life, liberty, and the pursuit of happiness."

Our determination to believe in a single logically complete theory as our heritage from the earliest settlers has thus actually kept us from grasping the *facts* of the early life of our nation. Strenuous efforts have been made to homogenize all the fathers of our country. A great deal of the popular misunderstanding of the New England Puritans, for example, can be traced to this desire. Tradition teaches us to treat the history of our nation from 1620 to 1789 as a series of labor pains, varying only in intensity. The Puritans, we are taught, came here for religious and political liberty; and the American Revolutionaries are supposed to have shown a pilgrim-like fervor and clarity of purpose.

If we compare our point of view with that of the historically conscious peoples of Europe, we shall begin to see some of its implications. The Europeans have, of course, had their interludes of nostalgia for some mythical heroic age, some Wagnerian Götterdämmerung. Mussolini sought to reincarnate the Roman Empire, Hitler to revive some prehistoric "Aryan" community. But such efforts in Europe have been spasmodic. Europeans have not with any continuity attributed to their nameless "earliest settlers" the mature ideals of their national life. In contrast, we have been consistently primitivistic. The brevity of our history has made this way of thinking easy. Yet that is not the whole story. We find it peculiarly congenial to claim possession of a perfect set of political ideas, especially when they have magical elusiveness and flexibility. Their mere existence seems to relieve us of an unwelcome task.

Our firm belief in a perfectly preformed theory helps us understand many things about ourselves. In particular, it helps us see how it has been that, while we in the United States have been unfertile in political theories, we have at the same time possessed an overweening sense of orthodoxy. The poverty of later theorizing has encouraged appeal to what we like to believe went before. In building an orthodoxy from sparse materials, of necessity we have left the penumbra of heresy vague. The inarticulate character of American political theory has thus actually facilitated heresy-hunts and tended to make them indiscriminate. The heresy-hunts which come at periods of national fear—the Alien and Sedition Acts of the age of the French Revolution, the Palmer raids of the age of the Russian Revolution, and similar activities of more recent times—are directed not so much against acts of espionage as against acts of irreverence toward that orthodox American creed, believed to have been born with the nation itself.

Among the factors which have induced us to presuppose an orthodoxy, to construct what I have called a "preformation" theory, none has been more important than the heterogeneous character of our population. Our immigrants, who have often been the outcasts, the déclassés, and the persecuted of their native countries, are understandably anxious to become part of a new national life. Hence they are eager to believe that they can find here a simplicity of theory lacking in the countries from which they came. Immigrants, often stupidly blamed for breeding "subversive" or "un-American" ideas, have as much as any other group frenetically sought a "pure" American doctrine. Where else has there been such a naïve sense of political orthodoxy? Who would think of using the word "un-Italian" or "un-French" as we use the word "un-American"?

Why a Theory Seems Needless

The fact that we have had a written constitution, and even our special way of interpreting it, has contributed to the "preformation" notion. Changes in our policy or our institutions are read back into the ideas, and sometimes into the very words, of the Founding Fathers. Everybody knows that this had made of our federal Constitution an "unwritten" document. What is more significant is the way in which we have justified the adaptation of the document to current needs: by attributing clarity, comprehensiveness, and a kind of mystical foresight to the social theory of the founders. In Great Britain, where there is an "unwritten" constitution in a very different sense, constitutional theory has taken for granted the *gradual* formulation of a theory of society. No sensible Briton would say that his history is the unfolding of the truths implicit in Magna Charta and the Bill of Rights. Such documents are seen as only single steps in a continuing process of definition.

The difference is expressed in the attitudes of the highest courts in the two countries. In Great Britain the highest court of appeal, the House of Lords, has gradually come to the conclusion that it must be governed by its own earlier decisions. When the House of Lords decides a point of the constitution, it is thus frankly developing the constitution, and it must follow the line which it has previously taken, until the legislature marks out another. Not so in the United States. Our Supreme Court considers itself free to overrule its earlier decisions, to discover, that is, that the constitution which it is interpreting really has all along had a different meaning from what had been supposed.

The American view is actually closer to the British view during the Middle Ages, when the very idea of legislation was in its infancy and when each generation believed that it could do little more than increase its knowledge of the customs which already existed. In the United States, therefore, we see the strange fact that the more flexible we have made our constitution, the more rigid and unexperimental we have made our political theory. We are haunted by a fear that capricious changes in theory might imperil our institutions. This is our kind of conservatism.

Our theory of society is thus conceived as a kind of exoskeleton, like the shell of the lobster. We think of ourselves as growing *into* our skeleton, filling it out with the experience and resources of recent ages. But we always suppose that the outlines were rigidly drawn in the beginning. Our mission, then, is simply to demonstrate the truth—or rather the workability—of the original theory. This belief in a perfect original doctrine, one of the main qualities of which is practicality, may help us understand that unique combination of empiricism and idealism which has characterized American political life.

If we turn from our constitution to our political parties, we observe the same point of view. The authority of a particular past generation implies the impotence of later generations to reconstruct the theoretical bases of our national life. Today it is still taken for granted that the proper arena of controversy was marked off once and for all in the late eighteenth century: we are either Jeffersonians or Hamiltonians.

In no other country has the hagiography of politics been more important. The lives of our national saints have remained vivid and contemporary for us. In no other country—except perhaps in Soviet Russia, where people are called Marxists, Leninists, or Trotskyites—do statesmen so intimately embrace the image of early national heroes. Would an Englishman call himself a Walpolean or a Pittite? Yet in the United States the very names of our political parties—Republican and Democratic—are borrowed from the early age of our national life. This remarkable persistence of early labels offers the sharpest contrast to what we see in continental western Europe. There new parties—and new party labels—come and go with the seasons, and most of the parties, with double- or triple-barreled names, draw on the novel vocabulary of the nineteenth and twentieth centuries. It is a commonplace that no fundamental theoretical difference separates our American political parties. What need has either party for an explicit political theory when both must be spokesmen of the *original* American doctrine on which the nation was founded?

Political theory has been little studied in the United States. For example, departments of political science in many of our universities show more interest in almost anything else than in political theory. This, too, can be explained in part by the limitations imposed by the "preformation" point of view. If our nation in the beginning was actually founded on an adequate and sufficiently explicit theory revealed at one time, later theorists can have only the minor task of exegesis, of explaining the sacred texts. Constitutional history can, and in many ways has, become a substitute for political theory.

The unique role which our national past has played in constructing our image of ourselves and our standards for American life has made us hypersensitive about our own history. Because we have searched it for the substance of a political philosophy, we have been inclined to exaggerate its contemporary relevance. When Charles A. Beard in his *Economic Interpretation of the Constitution* in 1913 showed that members of the Constitutional Convention had a financial interest in the establishment of a stable federal government, he scandalized respectable scholars. Leaders of opinion, like Nicholas Murray Butler, thought the book a wholesale attack on the American creed. The explosive import of such a book would have been impossible, had not the facts of political history already been elevated into an axiom of political philosophy. Any innuendo against the motives of the Founding Fathers was therefore seen as an implied attack on the American way of life. The British have never been so disturbed by the suggestion that the barons had a personal interest in extracting from King John the concessions written into Magna Charta.

During the 1930's, when the Communist party made a serious effort to appear a native American growth (using the slogan "Communism Is Twentieth-Century Americanism"), it too sought to reinterpret the American past. It argued that the American Revolution had really been a class war and not merely a colonial rebellion. The radical attack on the doctrine of judicial review, which then seemed to obstruct change in our institutions, was made by way of a labored two-volume historical treatise, Louis Boudin's *Government by Judiciary*. He sought to prove that the Founding Fathers had never intended the Supreme Court to have the power to declare federal laws unconstitutional.

The lives of our great men have played a peculiarly large role in our attempt at self-definition. Some of our best historical talent has in recent years gone into biography: Beveridge's *Marshall*, Van Doren's *Franklin*, Malone's *Jefferson*, and Freeman's *Washington*. We have also the long filial tradition of Sparks's or Weems's or Marshall's *Washington* or Wirt's *Patrick Henry*. Such works are a kind of hybrid between what the lives of the saints or of the Church Fathers are for Catholics and what the lives of gods and goddesses were for the ancient Greeks. For us, biographies have taken on a special importance, precisely because we have had so little dogmatic writing. And our national history thus has a primary significance for Americans which is without parallel in modern nations. The quest for the meaning of our political life has been carried on through historical rather than philosophical channels.

It is not surprising, then, that much of our self-criticism has taken the form of historical reinterpretation. In periods of disillusionment we have expressed ourselves not so much in new philosophies, in dogmas of dictatorship or existentialism, as in earnest, if sometimes tortured, reinterpretations of the American past. In the 1920's and 1930's, for example, people who would not have looked twice at a revolutionary political theory or a nihilist metaphysic eagerly read W. E. Woodward's *New American History*, James Truslow Adams' *Founding of New England*, Edgar Lee Masters' *Lincoln*, or the numerous other iconoclastic works about Washington or Grant. The sharpest criticisms of contemporary America were the works of Sinclair Lewis and H. L. Mencken, which were hardly theoretical.

The mystic rigidity of our "preformation" theory has been consistent with great flexibility in dealing with practical problems. Confident that the wisdom of the Founding Fathers somehow made provision for all future emergencies, we have not felt bound to limit our experiments to those which we could justify with theories in advance. In the last century or so, whenever the citizens of continental western Europe have found themselves in desperate circumstances, they have had to choose among political parties, each of which was committed to a particular theoretical foundation for its whole program— "monarchist," "liberal," "catholic," "socialist," "fascist," or "communist." This has not been the case in the United States. Not even during the Civil War: historians still argue over what, if any, political theory Lincoln represented. In the crisis which followed the great depression, when Franklin D. Roosevelt announced his program for saving the American economy, he did not promise to implement a theory. Rather, he declared frankly that he would try one thing after another and would keep trying until a cure was found. "The country demands bold, persistent experimentation. It is common sense to take a method and try it: if it fails, admit it frankly and try another." Neither he nor his listeners doubted that whatever solution, within the limits of common-law liberties, might prove successful would also prove to have been within the prevision of the Founding Fathers. The people balked only when a proposal—like the Court-packing plan—seemed to imperil the independence of the judiciary, an ancient principle of the common law.

On second thought, it is not surprising that we who have been most sure of the basic structure of our political life should also have been most prodigal of legislation. Two remarkable and complementary facts are that the amendments to our federal Constitution have been so few (only twelve in addition to the first ten amendments, or bill of rights) during the last century and a half, and that at the same time our legal experiments have been so numerous. For us it is enough to recommend a piece of legislation if a considerable number of people want it, if there is no loud opposition, and if there seems a reasonable chance that it might reduce some present evil. Our laws have been abundant and ephemeral as the flies of summer. Conservatism about our basic institutions, and the faith that they will be vindicated in the national experience, have made us less fearful of minor legislation.

Our mystic belief in the "preformed" national theory has thus restrained theoretical vagaries without preventing particular experiments. Without having ever intended it, we have thus stumbled on an evolutionary approach to institutions. Yet at the same time we have taken up a

plicit in the American experience. The idea that the American landscape is a giver of values is, of course, old and familiar. It has long been believed that in America the community values would not have to be sought through books, traditions, the messianic vision of prophets, or the speculative schemes of philosophers but would somehow be the gift of the continent itself.

We Americans have always been much impressed by the simple fact that we are children of a Brave New World. Even from the earliest settlements, but especially since the formative era of the late eighteenth and early nineteenth centuries, we have looked upon ourselves as the lucky beneficiaries of an especially happy environment. In the pamphlets which Puritans wrote in the seventeenth century to attract their brethren to New England, we read fantastic tales of the abundance of crops and game, the magic of the air and water; how life on the new continent cured consumption, gout, and all sorts of fevers; how the old became young, the young became vigorous, and barren women suddenly bore children. In the very same pamphlet we can read how the wilderness would toughen the effete and how the wealth of this unexploited paradise would enrich the impoverished.

The myth was no less alive two centuries later, when Paul Bunyan, the giant woodsman of the forest frontier (as James Stevens describes him),

felt amazed beyond words that the simple fact of entering Real America and becoming a Real American could make him feel so exalted, so pure, so noble, so good. And an indomitable conquering spirit had come to him also. He now felt that he could whip his weight in wildcats, that he could pull the clouds out of the sky, or chew up stones, or tell the whole world anything.

"Since becoming a Real American," roared Paul Bunyan, "I can look any man straight in the eye and tell him to go to hell! If I could meet a man of my own size, I'd prove this instantly. We may find such a man and celebrate our naturalization in a Real American manner. We shall see. Yay, Babe!"

Then the two great Real Americans leaped over the Border. Freedom and Inspiration and Uplift were in the very air of this country, and Babe and Paul Bunyan got more noble feelings in every breath [*Paul Bunyan* (New York, 1948), pp. 27 f.].

We have been told again and again, with the metaphorical precision of poetry, that the United States is the *land* of the free. Independence, equality, and liberty, we like to believe, are breathed in with our very air. No nation has been readier to identify its values with the peculiar conditions of its landscape: we believe in *American* equality, *American* liberty, *American* democracy, or, in sum, the *American* way of life.

Our belief in the mystical power of our land has in this roundabout way nourished an empirical point of view; and a naturalistic approach to values has thus, in the United States, been bound up with patriotism itself. What the Europeans have seen as the gift of the past, Americans have seen as the gift of the present. What the European thinks he must learn from books, museums, and churches, from his culture and its monuments, the American thinks he can get from contemporary life, from seizing peculiarly American opportunities.

It is surely no accident that the most influential, if not the only significant, general interpretation of our history has been that of Frederick Jackson Turner. He found the special virtues of our institutions and of our national character in the uniquely recurrent conditions of our frontier. Turner translated Paul Bunyan into the language of sociology:

> Behind institutions, behind constitutional forms and modifications, lie the vital forces that call these organs into life and shape them to meet changing conditions. . . . All peoples show development. . . . But in the case of the United States we have a different phenomenon. . . . This perennial rebirth, this fluidity of American life, this expansion westward with its new opportunities, its continuous touch with the simplicity of primitive society, furnish the forces dominating American character [pp. 2 f.].
>
> The result is that to the frontier the American intellect owes its striking characteristics. That coarseness and strength combined with acuteness and inquisitiveness; that practical, inventive turn of mind, quick to find expedients; that masterful grasp of material things, lacking in the artistic but powerful to effect great ends; that restless, nervous energy; that dominant individualism, working for good and for evil, and withal that buoyancy and exuberance which comes with freedom—these are traits of the frontier, or traits called out elsewhere because of the existence of the frontier [*The Frontier in American History* (New York, 1920), p. 37].

These words—indeed, much of the work of Turner and his followers—are actually a theory to justify the absence of an American political theory.

How can we explain the origin, growth, and vitality of this idea of "givenness" in America? The most obvious and some of the most important explanations have escaped us for their very obviousness; to become aware of them it may be necessary to go to Europe, where some of us begin to discover America.

One fact which becomes increasingly difficult to communicate to the urban American, but which the automobile and our national parks have kept alive for some of us, is the remarkable grandeur of the American continent. Even for the early Puritan settlers the forest which hid savage arrows had a fascination. The magic of the land is a leitmotif throughout the eighteenth and nineteenth centuries. We hear it, for example, in Jefferson's ecstatic description of the confluence of the Potomac and the Shenandoah rivers; in Lewis and Clark's account of the far west; in the vivid pages of Francis Parkman's *Oregon Trail;* and in a thousand other places. It is echoed in the numberless travel-books and diaries of those men and women who left the comfortable and dingy metropolises of the Atlantic seaboard to explore the Rocky Mountains, the prairies, or the deserts. Their simple emotions should not be underestimated, nor should we interpret them with too much subtlety. It is misleading to associate too closely the appeal of virgin America with the bookish romanticism of European belles-lettres. The unspoiled grandeur of America helped men believe that here the Giver of values spoke to man more directly—in the language of experience rather than in that of books or monuments.

Our immigrant character has been an incentive toward this point of view. The United States has, of course, been peopled at widely distant times and for the most diverse reasons. Some came because they were Protestants, others because they were Catholics, still others because they were Jews; some because they were monarchists, others because they were opposed to monarchy. We have been too well aware of this diversity to try to seek our common values in our original cultures. It is true, as I shall explain in my fifth chapter, that we have developed a kind of generalized Christianity, which is probably what we mean by the "In God We Trust" on our coins. We have looked anxiously for some common faith. A few writers, like Louis Adamic, have even tried to make the motleyness itself a scheme of values: to make the patchwork seem the pattern. But the readiest solution, a necessary solution, perhaps the only possible solution for us, has been to assume, in the immigrant's own phrase, that ours is a "golden land," that values spring from our common ground. If American ideals are not in books or in the blood but in the air, then they are readily acquired; actually, it is almost impossible for an immigrant to avoid acquiring them. He is not required to learn a philosophy so much as to rid his lungs of the air of Europe.

The very commonness of American values has seemed their proof: they have come directly from the hand of God and from the soil of the continent. This attitude helps explain why the martyr (at least the *secular* martyr) has not been attractive to us. In the accurate words of our popular song, "The Best Things in Life Are Free." Men in America have had to struggle against nature, against wild Indians, high mountains, arid deserts, against space itself. But these struggles have seemed required to make the continent livable or comfortable, not to make our society good. In Europe, on the other hand, the liberal could not make the plant of liberty grow without first cutting out the weeds of tyranny; and he took that for his task. But the American has preened himself on his good sense in making *his* home where liberty is the natural growth. Voltaire declared, "Where liberty is not, there is my home." This was a fitting and thoroughly un-American reply to Franklin's "Where liberty dwells, there is my country."

The character of our national heroes bears witness to our belief in "givenness," our preference for the man who seizes his God-given opportunities over him who pursues a great private vision. Perhaps never before has there been such a thorough identification of normality and virtue. A "red-blooded" American must be a virtuous American; and nearly all our national heroes have been red-blooded, outdoor types who might have made the varsity team. Our ideal is at the opposite pole from that of a German Superman or an irredentist agitator in his garret. We admire not the monstrous but the normal, not the herald of a new age but the embodiment of his own. In the language of John Dewey, he is the well-adjusted man; in the language of Arthur Miller's Salesman, Willy Loman, he is the man who is not merely liked but *well*-liked. Our national heroes have not been erratic geniuses like Michelangelo or Cromwell or Napoleon but rather men like Washington and Jackson and Lincoln, who possessed the commonplace virtues to an extraordinary degree.

III. THE CONTINUITY OF AMERICAN HISTORY

The third part of the idea of "givenness," as I have said, is actually a kind of link between the two axioms which I have already described: the notion that we have an ideal given in a particular period in the past (what I have called the idea of "preformation") and the idea that the theory of American life is always being given anew in the present, that values are implicit in the American experience. The third aspect to which I now turn helps us understand how we can at once appeal to the past and yet be fervently unhistorical in our approach to it.

By this I mean the remarkable continuity or homogeneity of American history. To grasp it, we must at the outset discard a European cliché about us, namely, that ours is a land without continuity or tradition, while in Europe man feels close to his ancestors. The truth of the matter is that anyone who goes to Europe nowadays cannot fail to be impressed with the amazing, the unique, continuity of American history and, in sharp contrast, the *dis*continuity of European history.

This is true in several senses. In the first place, there is the obvious fact that the recent history of Europe has seen violent oscillations of regime. Each new regime has taken on itself a task of historical amnesia: the fascists trying to deny their democratic past, the democrats trying to deny their fascist past, etc. But there is a subtler way in which the landscape and monuments which surround the European tend to impress on him the various possibilities of life in his place, while what the American sees confirms his sense of "givenness," his belief in the normality, if not the inevitability, of the particular institutions which he has evolved. "For the American tourist," Aldous Huxley has shrewdly observed, "the greatest charm of foreign travel is the very high ratio of European history to European geography. Conversely, for the European, who has come to feel the oppressive weight of a doubtless splendid, but often fatal past, the greatest charm of travel in the New World is the high ratio of its geography to its history."

Let me explain. I have recently been abroad, where I spent the better part of a year in Italy. My impressions there sharpened that contrast which I have been describing between the American and the European image of the past. The first church I visited was the Capella Palatina in Palermo, where Christian mosaics of the twelfth century are surmounted by a ceiling of Moslem craftsmanship. Throughout Sicily one comes upon pagan temples on the foundations of which rose churches, in the Middle Ages transformed into mosques, later again to be used as Christian chapels.

The capitals of Europe are rich in evidence of the unpredictability of human history. Of all cities in the world, Rome is perhaps richest in such evidence: the retaining walls which early Romans built to protect the road up the Palatine are made of fragments stolen from Greek and North African temples; columns standing in the Forum bear witness not only to ancient Roman skill but also to the shattered schemes of the conquered peoples from whom they were taken. The fate which the Romans brought upon their predecessors was later, of course, visited upon Rome herself by the barbarians and Christians, who made the Forum into their stone-quarry. The

Colosseum, where Christians and Jews were once slaugh-
tered to amuse the mob, is now divided by partitions
which later Christians erected to support the stage of
their Passion Play. Its walls are pocked by holes from
which barbarian and Christian soldiers extracted iron for
their weapons in the Middle Ages; large segments were
removed by popes to add splendor to their churches. The
magnificent roads which Julius Caesar built for his legions
are traveled by little automobiles which, with appropriate
irony, borrow their name from "Mickey Mouse"—in
Italian, "Topolino."

In Europe one need not be an archeologist or a philosopher to see that over the centuries many different kinds
of life are possible in the same place and for the same
people. Who can decide which, if any of these, is "normal" for Italy? It is hardly surprising, then, that the people of Europe have not found it easy to believe that their
values are given by their landscape. They look to ideology to help them choose among alternatives.

In the United States, of course, we see no Colosseum,
no Capella Palatina, no ancient roads. The effect of this
simple fact on our aesthetic sense, though much talked
of, is probably less significant than on our sense of history
and our approach to values. We see very few monuments
to the uncertainties, the motley possibilities, of history or,
for that matter, to the rise and fall of grand theories of
society. Our main public buildings were erected for much
the same purpose for which they are now being used.
The Congress of the United States is still housed in the
first building expressly constructed for that purpose. Al-

though the White House, like the Capitol, was gutted by fire during the War of 1812, it, too, was soon rebuilt on the same spot and to a similar design; in 1952 another restoration was completed. Our rural landscape, with a few scattered exceptions—the decayed plantation mansions of the South, the manor houses of upstate New York, and the missions of Florida and California—teaches us very little of the fortunes of history. Even our archeology is republican, designed to make the past contemporary; you can spend a vacation at Colonial Williamsburg.

The impression which the American has as he looks about him is one of the inevitability of the particular institutions, the particular kind of society in which he lives. The kind of acceptance of institutions as proper to their time and place which tyrants have labored in vain to produce has in the United States been the result of the accidents of history. The limitations of our history have perhaps confined our philosophical imagination; but they have at the same time confirmed our sense of the continuity of our past and made the definitions of philosophers seem less urgent. We Americans are reared with a feeling for the unity of our history and an unprecedented belief in the normality of our kind of life to our place on earth.

We have just been observing that our history has had a continuity: that is, that the same political institutions have persisted throughout our whole national career and therefore have acquired a certain appearance of normality and inevitableness. No less important is the converse of this fact, namely, that our history has *not* been *dis*continuous, has not been punctuated by the kind of internal struggles which have marked the history of most of the countries of western Europe, and which have fed their awareness that society is shaped by men. Two apparent exceptions to this observation are the American Revolution and the Civil War, with which I shall deal in later chapters. The important fact is what De Tocqueville observed a century ago, namely, that America somehow has reaped the fruits of the long democratic revolution in Europe "without having had the revolution itself." This was but another way of saying that the prize for which Europeans would have to shed blood would seem the free native birthright of Americans.

During these last one hundred and seventy-five years the history of the United States has thus had a unity and coherence unknown in Europe. Many factors—our geographical isolation, our special opportunities for expansion and exploitation within our own borders, and our remoteness from Europe—have, of course, contributed. Even our American Civil War, which shook us deeply and was one of the bloodiest wars anywhere in the century, can be understood with scant reference to the ideologies then sweeping Europe: to the intellectual background of 1848, of the Risorgimento, of the Paris Commune. It was not properly a counterpart of European struggles of the period, nor really an exception to the domestic continuity of our history.

But, whatever the causes, the winds of dogma and the gusts of revolution which during the last century and a half have blown violently over western Europe, making France, Italy, Germany, and now perhaps even England testing grounds for panaceas, have not ruffled our intellectual climate. The United States, with a kind of obstinate provincialism, has enjoyed relatively calm weather. While European politics became a kaleidoscope, political life in the United States has seemed to remain a window through which we can look at the life envisaged by our patriarchs. The hills and valleys of European history in the nineteenth century have had no real counterpart in the history of the United States. Because our road has been relatively smooth, we have easily believed that we have trod no historical road at all. We seem the direct beneficiaries of our climate, our soil, and our mineral wealth.

II

THE PURITANS: FROM PROVIDENCE
TO PRIDE

THE forces which have led us to seek our values in our land rather than in our philosophy have been numerous and can be traced back to the earliest period of settlement. The experience of the New England Puritans, despite its remoteness, is among the most instructive episodes of our history for helping us understand the place of theory in American political life. For the Puritans were the first, and perhaps the last, sizable community in American history to import from Europe a fully developed and explicit social dogma, and to try to live by it on this continent. The fate of Puritanism in America thus gives us our unique opportunity to see what kind of success and what kind of failure a self-conscious and comprehensive theory has actually met here.

If ever there was a dogma fit to arm a weak settlement on a savage frontier, it was Puritanism. And yet the very success of the Puritan community on that frontier was to be the undoing of their philosophy. Their success induced them gradually to seek their standards in their own experience, to make what they had accomplished the yardstick of what they might have, or ought to have, accomplished. We shall see how the pragmatic spirit, the belief in "givenness," seeped into the interstices of the Puritan dogma and was gradually to dissolve it into a more general faith in the magical definition of American purpose out of the American success.

It is doubtful if there has ever anywhere been a more subtle, a more comprehensive, or more beautifully put-together theory of society than that which the Pilgrims and Puritans brought with them in the early seventeenth century. One of its marvels was that it was equally capable of communication in heavy treatises like William Ames's *Marrow of Sacred Divinity* and in five-minute talks like John Winthrop's speech to the General Court. It was a miracle of logic, with its own way of asking and of answering any question you might put. Of all people in modern history, these early Puritans could be least accused of confusion about their ends or of that inarticulateness which I have described as a characteristic of American political thought. These people were eager to tell why they were here, what their community was about, and where they were going. The Pilgrims came to the New World, William Bradford explains in his *History*, "not out of any newfanglednes, or other such like giddie humor, by which men are oftentimes transported to their great hurt and danger, but for sundrie weightie and solid reasons."

Not only did the early settlers come to New England with an explicit philosophy, but their philosophy, as I shall try to show, had characteristics which fitted it ad-

37

mirably to be a prop for people struggling in the wilderness. In the very beginning, at least, the American experience, far from corroding Puritan dogma, actually seemed its strongest possible proof. For a while, New England would give a dazzling vividness to their dogma. But only in the beginning. For, as the Puritans threw themselves into the struggle against nature, developed their equipment for that struggle, and finally succeeded in building Zion in the wilderness, they were increasingly subject to those influences which were to persist in American history. We can see the growing sense of "givenness," the growing tendency to make the "is" the guide to the "ought," to make America as it was (or as they had now made it) a criterion of what America ought to be. This was the breakdown of classic Puritanism which I have called the movement from providence to pride.

We all know, of course, that Puritanism was a European product, brought here in its nearly finished state. We also know that Puritan orthodoxy, even in Europe, was not to outlive the seventeenth century; that many causes—among others, the growth of science, of rationalism, of materialism, of skepticism, and of evangelical religion—later led in Europe to the breakdown of what had once been a rounded theory of society. What was to be characteristic of American thought was not the fact that the Puritan theory broke down. Puritanism had a comprehensiveness, a brittleness, and a symmetry which destined it for a brief life anywhere. What was characteristic here was not *that* it broke down, but *how*.

The Puritan experience in America was to be distin-

guished by at least two features: first, an impressive success against great obstacles, the sudden building of new
communities and new institutions; and second, a direct
encounter with nature. Because the dogma which the
Puritans brought with them was so sophisticated, complete, and articulate and because the America against
which they struggled was so virginal, wild, and prehistoric, the pressures toward a sense of "givenness" appear
with extraordinary clarity in the story of their American
community. The anachronism which was to flavor much
of American history—the Bible in the wilderness and the
rifle against the tomahawk—would never be sharper.
Moreover, the sense of having made something of nothing, the awe before a paleolithic landscape which could
suddenly sprout civilized communities, would never be
more poignant than it must have been in that age.

In the sin of "pride" the Puritans were to have a perfect word for describing the temptations of their success.
It is, I believe, a French (and not an American) proverb
that "Nothing succeeds like success." While we in the
United States have been accused of having a "success-
philosophy," the accusation can come only from a certain
crudeness in approaching our history. It might be more
accurate to say that our success has made us unphilo-
sophical; that a soil where new institutions flourish is not
likely to be fertile for metaphysics. Pride of accomplish-
ment has perhaps always and everywhere been a satisfying substitute for a metaphysic of victory.

Of all this, nothing could be more vivid proof than
the Puritan experience in its first generations in New

England. The success of man's practical energies and the continuity of his institutions were to characterize American history and to make the American increasingly indifferent to cosmic dogmas while he came to believe that his task and his purpose were given by the land in which he lived. In this the Puritans were to foreshadow the way of American political thought.

I. THE WILDERNESS CONFIRMS PURITANISM

If anyone had tried to make of whole cloth a philosophy to fortify a weak community on a wild continent, he could hardly have done better than to invent what the Puritans actually brought with them. A disillusioned, indolent, or cowardly Puritan was a contradiction in terms. Works like Norton's *Orthodox Evangelist* or the sermons of Thomas Shepard and John Cotton provided a marvelous combination: optimism and a sense of mission derived from faith that they were the chosen people of God; pessimism coming from a belief in original sin and the weakness of man. Thus they were sure of their success, but neither surprised nor disappointed by their failures.

This character of their thought is pretty obvious. What is perhaps less obvious is that if the Puritans had been able to conjure up a *land* to demonstrate the truth of their theories—a proving-ground, as it were, for their theology —they could hardly have done better than to create the America which they found in the years just after 1620. They saw themselves abandoning the idolatry of the Egyptians in order to rebuild Zion: God's chosen people being led into the wilderness. But for them the line between fact and symbol was never clear; although they possessed an elaborate theory of symbolism—of "types" and "antitypes," in their phrase—they always felt more comfortable if they could see in daily experience the literal counterparts of biblical doctrine. Into a wilderness, then, it was proper for them to be led: no metaphorical wilderness where the perils would be the seven deadly sins, but a wilderness of dark woods, howling wolves, treacherous swamps, and barbarous savages. Such a wilderness the New World provided.

For their purposes the emptiness and isolation of the place would be an advantage, if not actually a necessity. When the Pilgrims first left England, they had gone not to America, but to Holland, where for about ten years they had sought to reconstruct Zion. Before coming to America, they had thus already made an extensive experiment of building a purified community within a corrupt society. As William Bradford recalled their experience in Holland:

That which was more lamentable, and of all sorowes most heavie to be borne, was that many of their children, by these occasions, and the great licentiousness of youth in that countrie, and the manifold temptations of the place, were drawne away by evill examples into extravagante and dangerous courses, getting the raines off their neks, and departing from their parents. Some became souldiers, others tooke upon them farr viages by sea, and other some worse courses, tending to dissolutnes and the danger of their soules, to the great greefe of their parents and dishonour of God. So that they saw their posteritie would be in danger to degenerate and be corrupted [*History of Plymouth Plantation* (New York, 1908), p. 46].

41

All about them in Europe they had found heresy and corruption. Their best and only hope was to escape altogether from civilization to some place where they would feel no pressure to compromise and where their children would be safe from evil example.

That they would have to pay a price for this opportunity, at least the better-informed of their leaders were well aware. Bradford, for example, knew that America was "vast and unpeopled . . . being devoyd of all civill inhabitants, wher ther are only salvage and brutish men, which range up and downe, litle otherwise then the wild beasts of the same." To build Zion in their age, they could perhaps do nothing better than actually to seek out "a hidious and desolate wildernes, full of wild beasts and willd men."

From the point of view of Puritan morality, there would be many subsidiary advantages in their new situation. Where better could men obey God's commandment to fill the earth with his people and his truth? John White, among others, who labored hard from the English side to prepare for the planting of the Colony of Massachusetts Bay, rejoiced at the magnificent way in which men could now advance "the respect unto Gods honor . . . by this worke of replenishing the earth." Here in new parts of the world men could taste "the largeness of his bounty" and discover "the extent of his munificence to the sonnes of men." The hardships and poverty of the new land would actually enlarge the scope for social virtues:

The Puritans: From Providence to Pride

That the spirits and hearts of men are kept in better temper by spreading wide, and by pouring, as it were, from vessell to vessell ... will [be] euident to any man, that shall consider, that the husbanding of unmanured grounds, and shifting into empty Lands, enforceth men to frugalitie, and quickneth invention: and the setling of new States requireth justice and affection to the common good: and the taking in of large Countreys presents a naturall remedy against couetousnesse, fraud, and violence; when euery man may enjoy enough without wrong or injury to his neighbour [White, "Planters Plea," in Peter Force, *Tracts* (New York, 1947), II, 3].

Not the least of the theological qualifications of the American continent would be the presence of the Indian savages. A completely uninhabited wilderness would not have served the mission of the Puritans so well as a land like America, peopled by a scattering of pagan tribes. In the first places, of course, the Indians would provide targets for their proselytizing zeal. The charter of the Massachusetts Bay Colony in 1629 declared that to "wynn and incite the Natives of [the] Country, to the Knowledg and Obedience of the onlie true God and Sauior of Mankinde, and the Christian Fayth . . . in our Royall Intencon, and the Adventurers free Profession, is the principall Ende of this Plantacion." Nor was this all. In a number of less obvious ways the Indians dramatized the social theory of the colonists.

Puritan theology, we should remember, depicted life on this earth as an unremitting struggle between God and Satan. Good Christians were soldiers in Christ's army battling against the forces of the Devil. Both in England and America, Puritans were, to be sure, quick to see this struggle in the minutiae of daily life. When Michael

43

Wigglesworth sat in his study in Cambridge in Massachusetts Bay and heard the wind slamming his neighbor's door, he tortured himself over whether God had intended him to disturb his thoughts to help a neighbor. Was Satan seducing him by the comforts of his study chair? Such English works as Richard Baxter's autobiography and the numerous collections of "cases of conscience" show how a conscientious Puritan could find cosmic issues in a sneeze.

The struggle between Christ and Satan was the daily meat and drink of Puritans. In England the Puritans had fought their good fight by defending one side of a sophisticated theological debate. In America, however, the Devil would seek special means to harry and discredit God's chosen. "The Divell," Bradford conjectured, "may carrie a greater spite against the churches of Christ and the gospell hear [in America], by how much the more they indeaour to preserve holynes and puritie amongst them." In the New World, Satan had cohorts worthy of him: the wild Indians.

According to reports which most of the Puritans believed, the Indians were cannibals, polygamists, and idolators; they were idle, showed no respect for property, lightly broke their treaties, and delighted in torturing their enemies. However vividly the Puritan ministers may have painted Laud as the champion of Satan, they could not but see Satan with a new vividness when he was championed by a band of pillaging Indians. These, in White's phrase, were the very "bond-slaves of Sathan." No theological education, no prayer-book learning, no knowledge of history was required to see that the savage must be the soldier of Anti-Christ. As the Indians were so obviously the soldiers of darkness, the daily struggle of the New England Puritan was not merely an effort to survive; in fact, he could survive only by defeating Evil.

The Puritan missionaries to the Indians do not marvel— as we might—that the Indians were reluctant to abandon their superstitions for European science. To Puritan eyes the Indians seemed anything but weak: were they not equipped with the powers of Satan? Major General Daniel Gookin, who was for many years superintendent of Indians for the Massachusetts Bay Colony, tells of a savage whose wife, in the toils of a difficult childbirth, had been offered the assistance of the native medicine man. Gookin finally persuaded the Indian to renounce the aid of his witch doctor and, instead, to pray to God; he is, of course, full of praise for the young Indian. But Gookin does not praise the savage for his prudence in giving up the ineffective hocus-pocus of a witch doctor in order to save his wife by civilized methods. Not at all; Gookin does not for one moment doubt the power of Satan. He praises the converted Indian, rather, all the more because he is willing to give up the sure assistance of Satan and so risk the unpredictability of God's will. If, indeed, the Puritans had conceived themselves as carriers of a White Man's Burden, as engaged in civilizing the Indians, they might have been discouraged. But this was not their purpose; and the more hostile and obstinate the Indians, the more assured were the Puritans of the need to redouble their efforts.

The period I have been speaking about is what I shall call the "classic" age of New England Puritanism. It is the age dominated by first-generation immigrants, that is, until about 1660 or 1670. In interpreting their own history in this classic age in New England, the Puritans leaned especially heavily on their *doctrine of providence*. While not ostensibly a philosophy of history, this doctrine was at least a satisfactory substitute for one. And perhaps the most remarkable of those coincidences by which the New World at first confirmed the dogmas of Puritanism was the way in which life in America substantiated this particular notion. For them it was the doctrine of providence that held together the commonplace and the extraordinary, the understood and the mysterious, showing the place of all events in the divine design for their community. "Actual Providence," Norton explained, "is that transient acting of God, whereby he upholdeth, and infallibly governeth all things, and the several natures of things according to the immutable Counsel of his own Will unto their best end, namely, the Manifestation of his own Glory."

Providence, in its most general sense, included all the everyday ways in which God fulfilled his design. The more dramatic aspect of providence, however, was not in the familiar tenor of life but rather in the extraordinary interventions of God to attain his ends. These the Puritans were accustomed to call "special" or "remarkable" or "illustrious" providences; and the ministers of Massachusetts Bay Colony defined them in the following fashion:

46

The Puritans: From Providence to Pride

Such Divine judgements, tempests, floods, earthquakes, thunders as are unusual, strange apparitions, or whatever else shall happen that is prodigious, witchcrafts, diabolical possessions, remarkable judgements upon noted sinners, eminent deliverances, and answers of prayer, are to be reckoned among illustrious providences [Declaration of ministers in general meeting, May 12, 1681, in Preface to I. Mather's *Remarkable Providences* (London, 1856)].

Like all of us, the Puritan saw God's hand less vividly in the beating of his own heart than in the lightning and the thunder.

America in that earliest Puritan age actually offered the best possible stage to show men the hand of God in human experience. In America everything was extraordinary.

In the first place, there was something extraordinary about the appearance within the European orbit of a continent which for millennia had been unknown to the civilized world. Just then North America was discovered (in De Tocqueville's phrase) "as if it had been kept in reserve by the Deity and had just risen from beneath the waters of the Deluge." What had been God's purpose in concealing the vast American continent from European eyes until so long after the Creation? Moreover, what was God's purpose in suddenly revealing this continent, in making it accessible in their particular epoch?

What shall we conceive of that almost miraculous opening the passage unto, and discovery of these formerly unknowne nations, which must needs have proved impossible unto former ages for want of the knowledge of the use of the Loadstone, as wounderfully found out as these unknowne Countries by it. It

47

were little lesse then impietie to conceive that GOD, (whose Will concurres with the lighting of a Sparrow upon the ground) had no hand in directing one of the most difficult and observeable workes of this age; and as great folly to imagine, that hee who made all things, and consequently orders and directs them to his owne glory, had no other scope but the satisfying of mens greedy appetites [White, "Planters Plea," in Force, *Tracts*, II, 8 f.].

But this was only the first of many providential facts which surrounded the early Puritan.

His very presence in America seemed nothing less than a remarkable providence. None of the first generation of Puritans of whom we are now speaking would have been in the New World unless he had survived the perils of a 3,000-mile sea voyage. Even supposing that romantic historians may have exaggerated, the perils of such voyages in the seventeenth century were far from negligible. An Englishman who found himself safely on American shores before 1650 must have been especially insensitive not to have seen something providential in his safe passage. God must have approved the Puritan mission in advance by giving favorable winds, stilling the sea, and moderating the weather. The collection of "illustrious providences" made by Increase Mather in 1684 in New England significantly opens with a chapter of "remarkable sea-deliverances." Every immigrant to early New England must at some time or other have felt the sentiments which William Bradford described at the first landing of the Pilgrims. "Being thus arived in a good harbor and brought safe to land, they fell upon their knees and blessed the God of heaven, who had brought them over the vast and furious ocean, and delivered them from all the periles and miseries thereof, againe to set their feete on the firme and stable earth, their proper elemente."

After the Puritans' arrival in their new haven, everything was calculated to sharpen their sense of providence, to emphasize God's special concern for them and their community. Where so little was known, few things could seem ordinary. We can see from their journals and diaries that everyday things now took on an air of the miraculous: the weather, a walk in the woods, finding one's way to a neighboring village. These were no longer the familiar acts of generations, as they had been in England. Now they were full of threats and surprises, all of which gave new force to the belief in providence. During those earliest years the Puritans report the weather as if it was the most unknown—as it was perhaps the most important—fact that confronted them. Being unfamiliar with the New England seasons, they saw a heavy snow as a visitation of God and a warm spring as his special blessing. The strange landscape, unexplained or misrepresented in their few maps, and the scarcity of even primitive roads made the trip from Boston to Cambridge (then Newtowne) a major adventure. John Winthrop's journal for these early years is full of accounts of men who started on a half-day journey, only to arrive at their destination bewildered and exhausted; of servants who went to the neighbor's house to borrow a pot, only to be lost for days in the woods. To undertake the simplest journey was to put one's self in the hands of providence: to arrive safely at any New England destination was to fall in debt to God.

The commonest plants and animals, simply because they were unfamiliar to European eyes, took on a providential aspect. If, in a season of famine, lobsters or oysters appeared in great number, this was an act of providence; if a flock of pigeons or ducks filled the heavens at a seasonable time, this, too, was a sign of God's care to feed his people. How were they to know that it was the regular lobster season in New England or that they had witnessed the annual bird migration along the Atlantic flyways? "What it portends I know not," Thomas Dudley wrote back to England in March, 1631, of the flocks of pigeons which crossed the New England skies in that month.

Against the Indians the settlers constantly required God's protection. "Thus it pleased God," Bradford recounts of the first Pilgrims' skirmish with the Indians "to vanquish their enimies and give them deliverance; and by his spetiall providence so to dispose that not any one of them were either hurte or hitt, though their arrows came close by them, and on every side them, and sundry of their coats, which hunge up in the barricado, were shot throw and throw. A[f]terwards they gave God sollamne thanks and praise for their deliverance, and gathered up a bundle of their arrows, and sente them into England."

They recalled the prophecy of Jesus in Matt. 24:27, where he described the progress of the gospel as the lightning that shone from the East into the West. "God meanes to carry his Gospel westward, in these latter times of the world," declared the author of *New England's First Fruits*, "and have thought, as the Sunne in the afternoon of the day, still declines more and more to the West, and then sets: so the Gospel (that great light of the world) though it rose in the East, and in former ages, hath lightened it with his beames; yet in the latter ages of the world will bend Westward, and before its setting, brighten these parts, with his glorious lustre also." That America was West thus became a dramatic coincidence. And even the points of the compass took on a theological import.

II. SUCCESS BRINGS THE DECLINE
OF PURITANISM

Until now I have been describing the ways in which the American experience seemed to confirm the Puritan dogma during the first generation in New England. Now I shall turn to the second and third generations, when we begin to see evidences of that attitude which I have described as a belief in "givenness." The growth of this attitude was, in the Puritan case, coincident with the decline of their particular dogma. It is well to recall, as I have already remarked, that the decline of Puritanism in New England was roughly contemporaneous with its decline in Old England, and with the Enlightenment's attack on traditional dogmas of all sorts. To be sure, the decline of any great philosophy must be the result of many causes. New England Puritans were in the currents —if sometimes only the backwaters—of European thought: their best minds were cosmopolitan, and there was always considerable movement of people and ideas between Old and New England. In one sense, the fate of Puritanism in America was of a piece with European history. Yet it would be a great mistake to allow the obvious cosmopolitan features of our history to obscure what was unique.

There were several unique features of the American story which are significant for our purpose. Among them is the fact that in the long run Puritanism in New England was to decline, not because it was defeated, but, in a sense, because it had succeeded. It was its spectacular success in building churches and communities, a success all the more spectacular because it was accomplished against the backdrop of what the Puritans themselves called a "howling wilderness," that led the Puritans to trust increasingly to their own energies and accomplishments, to find their purposes somehow implicit in their achievements.

For better or worse, there is a kind of continuity between the Harvard of Roger Conant of Salem (a member of the first committee appointed by the town in 1636 to view a site for an English university in New England) and the Harvard of James Bryant Conant. For in New England there was no proper counterpart to the English Restoration of 1660; no decisive defeat of the Puritans. If the dogma of Puritanism eventually declined, the influence of Puritans remained unbroken; at virtually every period in the later history of New England, dominant groups have claimed spiritual, as well as genealogical, descent from the Puritans of the classic age. This is but another example of the remarkable continuity of American history referred to in the first chapter and which we shall observe again and again. Puritanism in New England was not so much defeated by the dogmas of anti-Puritanism as it was simply assimilated to the conditions of life in America. Never was it blown away by a hurricane. It was gradually eroded by the American climate.

A distinctive and paradoxical feature of the American story was that the decline actually came in part from the removal of many of those perils which had earlier confirmed the Puritan dogmas. The more secure the Puritans became on this continent, the more meager and unimpressive became the daily proofs of their dogma. At the same time, success nourished their pride and gave them a community to which they could point as the embodiment of their philosophy. In all this we shall see how the New England story re-enacted one of the familiar ironies of history: in the very act of establishing their community, they undermined the philosophy on which it was to have been founded.

Just as the conditions of America in the first generation were admirably suited to confirm the Puritan beliefs, so the gradual removal of those conditions within the next generations was destined to undermine them. The firm establishment of a community in New England was marked by a growing sense of security, a decline of many of the fears and uncertainties which had nourished a desperate dependence on God. The second generation owed its presence in New England, not to God's happy guidance across the perils of an ocean, but to the simple accident of birth. Puritan immigrants who came after the mid-century were met, not by the Indian arrows which had greeted the first Pilgrims, but by the embrace of their countrymen. Glowing fireplaces and full storehouses were ready for them. Their welcome now seemed less from God—or from Satan—than from their fellow-Puritans.

The Indians were no longer such constant reminders of the powers of the Devil. The last great battle against them in the New England coastal settlements was King Philip's War (1675–76) when the Indians suffered disastrous defeat. Within a few decades, the savage population of Massachusetts Bay Colony had declined to an insignificant number. Puritan chroniclers record the fact with a mixture of sentimental remorse and hardheaded satisfaction. For, like all doctrinaires and fanatics, the Puritans had found it more difficult—and certainly less urgent—to convert their enemies than to exterminate them. Concern for their own young community had thus understandably stifled a lust for the souls of the unconverted. It is true that John Eliot, translator of the Bible into the Indian language, who was perhaps the most selfless, as he was surely the most successful, of the Puritan missionaries, had finally managed to convert a considerable band of Indians. But the Indians' only reward was deportation to a concentration camp on Deer Island.

As the fund of American experience increased, everyday events lost the magic of novelty and the mystery of the unexpected. More and more, life took on the air of the familiar, or even of the banal. The Puritans had now come to look for the bitter winter and the inspiriting spring of New England. The seasonal pattern of habits of the wild animals, the birds, and the fish was gradually discovered. Having learned the best ways of growing Indian corn, the Puritans saw more and more connection between their own efforts and the product of the soil. As they charted the Indian trails, named the hills, and followed the curves of the rivers, they built their own bridges and ferries and established the ways from one village to another. Now if one failed to reach his destination, he had to blame himself.

With remarkable rapidity the Puritans in New England built up their knowledge of the nature around them. The encyclopedic farmer's almanac displaced the catalogue of remarkable providences. As their interest in and mastery of natural history increased, New England Puritans—for example, Cotton Mather, John Leverett, Paul Dudley, John Winthrop, Jr., and Zabdiel Boylston—were enlisted in the Royal Society among the leaders of English science. In New England it was the clergy who propagated the new astronomy. The use of Charles Morton's *Compendium Physicae* and the growing laboratories of Harvard College attest the serious interest in what they called "experimental natural philosophy." Encouraged by the growing enthusiasm of their age for the laws of nature, they added nearly every day to the data of their science something which a few years before had been the stuff of theology.

In 1684, when Increase Mather wrote the Preface to

his collection of remarkable providences, he expressed his wish "that the Natural History of New-England might be written and published to the world; the rules and method described by that learned and excellent person Robert Boyle, Esq., being duely observed therein. It would best become some scholar that has been born in this land to do such a service for his countrey." Facts which formerly had been merely points of departure for the imaginative raconteur, or metaphors for sermons to exhort an isolated settlement, were gradually set in order. Now they had become useful knowledge. By the end of the seventeenth century the Puritans' familiarity with their environment, their increasing ability to predict the whims of the weather, and the gifts of the wilderness had seriously dulled—although it had not yet by any means destroyed—their sensitivity to the mysterious and the providential.

The development is nowhere clearer than in the striking change in the Puritan approach to their own history or, more precisely, in the growth of Puritan historical writing. The best early Pilgrim and Puritan accounts of themselves are contemporary chronicles, such as Bradford's history of Plymouth and John Winthrop's journal. These writings, and even lesser ones—like Johnson's *Wonder-working Providence of Sions Saviour in New England*—impress us with the Puritan's sense of his mission, his single-mindedness, his prudence, and his submission to the will of God. They are works of rare seriousness and dignity. But essentially they chronicle the fulfilment of a divine mission rather than the progress of a human enterprise. We are never allowed to forget that the principal protagonist is God, the enemy Satan; each is using men to attain his ends.

By the second or third generation in New England we note a change. It has sometimes been described as the appearance of a "modern" spirit in their historical writing. Now we begin to read works in which *men* are the protagonists: the reader's attention is focused on human successes and failures. Contemporary annals are replaced by retrospective history, dealing with causes and consequences. The discrete judgments of God—his dooms on the good and the evil—intelligible only in the light of cosmic and inscrutable purposes, now give way to the purposes of men.

At this period at the end of the seventeenth century, when the providential glow of the life of earliest New England was still a memory, there appeared the most important work of Puritan historiography, and indeed one of the greatest histories ever written in America. Cotton Mather's *Magnalia Christi Americana*, first published in 1702, was written while Puritan theology was sufficiently alive to give unity to a historical work; yet in its pages we encounter the first full flush of satisfaction at man's accomplishments in the New World. As Mather suggested in his title, he meant to focus on the achievements of Christ rather than on the providences of God. The *Magnalia* seems to tell us that God cannot be better glorified than by a display of the successes of the first two generations of his chosen people in the Wilderness. Here we begin to see the face of Pride.

We have considerable evidence, moreover, that the re-markable combination of piousness and complacency was no peculiarity of Mather, but was a general and growing sentiment. In his Preface to Mather's work, John Higginson writes:

> The Lord was pleased to grant such a gracious presence of his with them, and such a blessing upon their undertakings, that within a few years a wilderness was subdued before them, and so many Colonies planted, Towns erected, and Churches settled ... and that the Lord has added so many of the blessings of Heaven and earth for the comfortable subsistence of his people in these ends of the earth. . . . There is also a third generation, who are grown up, and begin to stand thick upon the stage of action, at this day, and these were all born in the country, and may call New-England their native land. Now, in respect of what the Lord hath done for these generations, succeeding one another, we have aboundant cause of Thanksgiving to the Lord our God, who hath so increased and blessed this people, that from a day of small things, he has brought us to be, what we now are.

The two heavy volumes of Mather's work seem them-selves to have been intended as a monument to the suc-cess which attends the orthodox. "So mighty was the work to found Christ's empire here," he boasts in the motto of his first book. Mather's prime interest is in "the *Actors*" and "the *Actions*"; his object is to recount "the design whereon, the manner wherein, and the people whereby, the several colonies of New-England were planted." In no other work of nationalist history—not even the writings of George Bancroft in the nineteenth century—can we find greater pride in the fortitude, wis-dom, and ingenuity of particular men. Mather deliberately chooses the form and even the phrase of epic, which is, after all, a tale of heroic adventure. He begins with a paraphrase of Virgil, "I write the Wonders of the Christian Religion, flying from the depravations of Europe, to the American Strand."

The epic parallel is never forgotten; the role of Aeneas and his Trojan warriors is played by John Winthrop and his faithful Puritans:

> Our New-England shall tell and boast of her Winthrop, a lawgiver as patient as Lycurgus, but not admitting any of his criminal disorders; as devout as Numa, but not liable to any of his heathenish madnesses, a governour in whom the excellencies of Christianity made a most improving addition unto the virtues, wherein even without those he would have made a parallel for the great men of Greece, or of Rome, which the pen of a Plutarch has eternized [*Magnalia* (Hartford, 1853), I, 118].

No one would have been more scandalized than Winthrop himself, to read such idolatry, such preening on the strength of mankind. Winthrop had seen himself as the instrument of God.

Mather is hardly to be blamed for pride in the work of his New England predecessors. Satisfaction was justified by the firm foundation of the churches and by the heroism of the New England fighters in "the wars of the Lord," as he called the battles against the Indians. It would have been surprising had Mather not sung the praises of Harvard College, which was already well established. He described his Alma Mater with his customary modesty, as "a river, without the streams whereof, these regions would have been meer unwatered places for the devil!" We could hardly ask for better evidence than Mather has provided us that, even for conservatives, the new security and prosperity of their community nourished a pride in the works of men. God, the providential guardian, who, for reasons best known to himself, had personally deflected the arrows of the Indians and had led the uncertain traveler by the hand from Boston to Cambridge—this God gradually slipped out of their vision. Instead, they began to see a beneficent Being who blessed their own human undertakings. They were moving from a sense of mystery to a consciousness of mastery; the two spirits could not well live together.

This movement was symbolized by a significant change in the character of New England holidays and religious festivals. For the first several decades after the arrival in New England, fast and thanksgiving days were unique occasions. If rain was lacking or an expected ship did not arrive, the magistrates would declare a day of fast to move God to their aid; if a good harvest was granted, a ship was saved from a storm, or the Indians were defeated in a battle, they would declare a day of thanksgiving and prayer. There was nothing regular or perfunctory about these occasions; they expressed the needs or the satisfaction felt by the community at a particular moment. A day of fast or thanksgiving in that earliest age did not mark the regular circuit of the calendar but was itself a symbol of the desperate unpredictableness of life in the wilderness.

By the third generation a significant, though not surprising, change had come over these institutions. Such occasions were now fixed by legislation, defined by the passage of a regular span of time or the recurrence of the season when the community had learned that it would be likely to have cause for thanksgiving. Inevitably, these holidays became symbols less of the prostration of the community before its Creator than of the solidarity of its members: a time for complacency. In this sense there could be nothing more un-Puritan than Thanksgiving Day, once the day had been fixed by law and the calendar rather than by the vicissitudes of life.

The sign of the times which was perhaps most characteristic of New England was the development of the so-called "Halfway Covenant." This doctrine signalized the acquiescence of the older divines in the decline of the sense of mystery and in the rise of a more naturalistic spirit in religion. Proposed by a New England Synod in 1662, it was not generally accepted in New England until some years later. The doctrine represented an abandonment of the strict concept of church membership which had characterized the first generation of Puritans.

According to that early doctrine, "membership" in the church (which they used in a special and technical sense) was one of the greatest mysteries. No one could be a member—that is, within the covenant himself—who had not had an experience of "regeneration" or of being saved. A child born of regenerate parents would, from that fact, be presumed to be holy and hence entitled to baptism; but this would not in itself give him full church membership. For that the personal "saving" experience was indispensable. This "saving" experience was neither the sure result of education nor a predictable response to any act of will. Rather it was an unforeseeable visitation of the spirit of God. Theologians might outline to the faithful some conditions which might prepare one to receive such an experience; and the faithful Puritan could, in a sense, prepare himself. But the experience itself remained mysterious. The arbitrariness with which God selected the men, the times, and the places for regeneration had become a symbol of that disparity between man's weakness and God's omnipotence which was at the heart of Puritan thought.

By the time of the second or third generation in New England, the Puritans, perhaps from an actual scarcity of such experiences, perhaps from a prudent unwillingness to leave the filling of church benches to the hand of providence, now redefined the concept of membership. Or, more precisely, they made an outspoken compromise on the way to abandoning the old mystery.

The Synod of 1662 proposed that henceforth those persons who had been baptized but had lacked the "saving experience" should be counted as "halfway" members of the church. Such membership would be sufficiently potent to be communicated in turn to their children also by the simple ceremony of baptism. In a word, the fact of individual membership (in the new diluted sense) and the size of the congregation would now admittedly be controlled by the community itself. By a devious and in some respects characteristically American route, they were finding their way back to one of those very doctrines from which they had wished to purify their English church. They had now come as close as they dared to making judgments for God. They had taken a long step in the direction of Solomon Stoddard (1643–1729), who a few years later was to argue in effect that all persons of good moral character be admissible to membership.

Men seemed more and more satisfied to show that they comprehended their world by the fact that they had come to master it. Philosophy—except to a lonely giant like Jonathan Edwards (1703–58)—seemed less impressive than institutions. Nor did the new spirit of mastery call forth any great philosophy of naturalism. Puritanism in earliest New England, as we have seen, had been rich in a sense of mystery. From one point of view, indeed, it had been little more than a way of formulating the unintelligibility of experience, of referring the most difficult issues—the salvation of the individual and the fate of the community—to the inscrutable and largely inaccessible purposes of God.

III. THE GROWING SENSE OF "GIVENNESS"

The declining sense of mystery which I have described carried with it an increasing directness in approaching all experience, a willingness to allow experience to give values. As the Puritan in the New World had come to feel that his enemies could be met and overcome, so he had come to feel less vividly the omnipresence of Satan. And as he came to discern and define his obstacles in the wilderness, so he was prepared to believe that even the fate of man's soul, the question of election itself—or at least of title to church membership—might not be entirely hidden from man.

No longer did he feel that he was encircled by enemies; rather he began to think of himself as confronting them. More and more of life seemed predictable, and the Puritan became ready to believe that perhaps the most important facts were intelligible to him, that he might read God's purpose in Nature's design. Once communities had become firmly established and wild men and wild animals had been exterminated from the gaps between the main coastal settlements, the Puritan community began to stand, or to feel that it stood, in a phalanx. With secure and prosperous communities behind them, men felt they could look outward from the larger centers to a definite line of battle in the West. Here, too, circumstances were to define the task.

There is no denying that the Puritan episode was in many ways untypical of later American experience: first, because the intellectual equipment of the earliest Puritans was so thoroughly European and, second, because the America they saw was virginal. By bringing Puritanism to America, they were, of course, starting the long process of importation of ideas from Europe. Their encounter with nature eventually helped disintegrate their original explicit philosophy. Their experience, of course, could not be precisely repeated in other frontier communities which were not equipped with any such explicit philosophy.

The mastery of nature depended on the ability to understand rather than on the ability to persuade. The Big

Lie could not help against a snowstorm; it would kill no wolves and grow no corn. Therefore, it was less important to make a grand plan, to make generalities glitter, than to know what was what and how to control the forces of nature. In mastering the wilderness, in building institutions and communities, the second and third generation of New England Puritans became somewhat less anxious to dot all the *I*'s and cross all the *T*'s in their theology. They became more and more responsive to the values which seemed to emerge from their daily lives. The Puritan experience thus shows some persistent characteristics of American history which have encouraged belief in the implicitness of values. Already in that earliest age we see a growing sense of "givenness."

There is a subtler sense in which the Puritan experience symbolizes the American approach to values. For the circumstances which have nourished man's sense of mastery over his *natural* environment have on this continent somehow led him away from dogmatism, from the attempt to plan and control the *social* environment. In this our history may have been distinctive. The two other nations in recent times which seem to have made a fetish of technology started in reverse order. The Nazis and Communists started with blueprints for society and turned to technology as the only means to attain their ends. For our political thought it has been a happy fact that the opposite was true. Nature had to be mastered before society could even survive.

III

THE AMERICAN REVOLUTION: REVOLUTION WITHOUT DOGMA

W E ARE accustomed to think of the Revolution as the great age of American political thought. It may therefore be something of a shock to realize that it did not produce in America a single important treatise on political theory. Men like Franklin and Jefferson, universal in their interests, active and spectacularly successful in developing institutions, were not fertile as political philosophers.

In the present chapter I shall offer some explanations of this fact and shall explore some of its significance for our later political life. I shall be trying to discover why, in the era of our Revolution, a political theory failed to be born. But my inquiry will not be entirely negative. I will seek those features of the Revolution, those positive ideas and attitudes, which actually have done much to reinforce our sense of "givenness."

We have been slow to see some of the more obvious and more important peculiarities of our Revolution because influential scholars on the subject have cast their story in the mold of the French Revolution of 1789. Some of our best historians have managed to empty our

Revolution of much of its local flavor by exaggerating what it had in common with that distinctively European struggle. This they have done in two ways.

First, they have stressed the international character of the intellectual movement of which the French Revolution was a classic expression—the so-called "Enlightenment." They speak of it as a "climate of opinion" whose effects, like the barometric pressure, could no more be escaped in America than in Europe. As Carl Becker put it in his *Heavenly City of the Eighteenth-Century Philosophers:* "The Enlightenment . . . is not a peculiarly French but an international climate of opinion . . . and in the new world Jefferson, whose sensitized mind picked up and transmitted every novel vibration in the intellectual air, and Franklin of Philadelphia, printer and friend of the human race—these also, whatever national or individual characteristics they may have exhibited, were true children of the Enlightenment. The philosophical empire was an international domain of which France was but the mother country and Paris the capital."

Second, they have treated ours as only a particular species of the genus "Revolution"—of what should perhaps more properly be called *revolutio Europaensis.* Since the French Revolution has been made the model, from that European revolution historians have borrowed the vocabulary in which ours is discussed and the calendar by which it is clocked. "Thermidor," for example, is the name used in one of our best college textbooks to introduce its chapter on the federal Constitution.

It goes on:

There comes a time in every revolutionary movement when the people become tired of agitation and long for peace and security. They then eliminate the radicals, trouble-makers and warmongers, and take measures to consolidate their government, hoping to secure what has already been gained through turmoil and suffering. *Thermidor* this time is called in leftist language, from the counter-revolution in France that overthrew Robespierre and ended the reign of terror. Thus, the establishment of Cromwell as Lord Protector was the Thermidor of the English Revolution in the seventeenth century; and the Stalin dictatorship and exile of Trotsky marks the Thermidor of the Russian Revolution. Every taking of the Bastille, it may be said, is inevitably followed by Thermidor, since human nature craves security, and the progress of a revolution must be stopped somewhere short of anarchy [Morison and Commager, *Growth of the American Republic* (3d ed.; New York, 1942), I, 277].

The effect of all this has been to emphasize—or rather exaggerate—the similarity of ours to all other modern revolutions.

In so doing, historians have exaggerated the significance of what is supposed to have been the ideology of the Revolution. Such an emphasis has had the further attraction to some "liberal" historians of seeming to put us in the main current of European history. It has never been quite clear to me why historians would not have found our revolution significant enough merely as a victory of constitutionalism.

I. SOME PECULIARITIES OF OUR REVOLUTION

The most obvious peculiarity of our American Revolution is that, in the modern European sense of the word, it was hardly a revolution at all. The Daughters of the

American Revolution, who have been understandably sensitive on this subject, have always insisted in their literature that the American Revolution was no revolution but merely a colonial rebellion. The more I have looked into the subject, the more convinced I have become of the wisdom of their naïveté. "The social condition and the Constitution of the Americans are democratic," De Tocqueville observed about a hundred years ago. "But they have not had a democratic revolution." This fact is surely one of the most important of our history.

A number of historians (J. Franklin Jameson and Merrill Jensen, for example) have pointed out the ways in which a social revolution, including a redistribution of property, accompanied the American Revolution. These are facts which no student of the period should neglect. Yet it seems to me that these historians have by no means succeeded in showing that such changes were so basic and so far-reaching as actually in themselves to have established our national republican institutions. When we speak of the Revolution therefore, we are still fully justified in referring to something other than what Jameson's disciples mean by "the American Revolution as a social movement." If we consider the American Revolution in that sense, it would not be a great deal more notable than a number of other social movements in our history, such as Jacksonianism, populism, progressivism, and the New Deal. Moreover, in so far as the American Revolution was a social movement, it was not much to be distinguished from European revolutions; and the increasing emphasis on this aspect of our history is but another example of the attempt to assimilate our history to that of Europe.

The Revolution, as the birthday of our nation, must mean something very different from all this. It is the series of events by which we separated ourselves from the British Empire and acquired a national identity. Looking at our Revolution from this point of view, what are some features which distinguish it from the French Revolution of 1789 or the other revolutions to which western European nations trace their national identity? And, especially, what are those peculiarities which have affected the place of theory in our political life?

1. First, and most important, the United States was born in a *colonial* rebellion. Our national birth certificate is a Declaration of Independence and not a Declaration of the Rights of Man. The vast significance of this simple fact is too often forgotten. Compared even with other colonial rebellions, the American Revolution is notably lacking in cultural self-consciousness and in any passion for national unity. The more familiar type of colonial rebellion—like that which recently occurred in India—is one in which a subject people vindicates its local culture against foreign rulers. But the American Revolution had very little of this character. On the contrary, ours was one of the few conservative colonial rebellions of modern times.

We should recall several of the peculiar circumstances (most of them obvious) which had made this kind of revolution possible. At the time of the Revolution, the major part of the population of the American colonies was of British stock. Therefore, no plausible racial or national argument could be found for the superiority either of the inhabitants of the mother-country or of the continental American colonies. Even when Jefferson, in his *Notes on Virginia*, went to some trouble to refute Buffon and the Abbé Raynal and others who had argued that all races, including man, deteriorated on the American continent, he did not go so far as to say that the American races were distinctly superior.

Since the climate and topography of substantial parts of the American colonies were similar to those of the mother-country (and for a number of other reasons), there had been a pretty wholesale transplantation of British legal and political institutions to North America. Unlike the Spanish colonies in South America, which were to rebel, at least in part, because they had had so little home rule, the British colonies in North America were to rebel because, among other reasons, they had had so much. Finally, the North American continent was (except for sparse Indian settlements) empty of indigenous populations, hence barren of such local institutions and traditions as could have competed with what the colonists had brought with them.

All these facts were to make it easy, then, for the American Revolution to seem in the minds of most of its leaders an affirmation of the tradition of British institutions. The argument of the best theorists of the Revolution—perhaps we should call them lawyers rather than theorists—was not, on the whole, that America had institutions or a culture superior to that of the British. Rather their position, often misrepresented and sometimes simply forgotten, was that the British by their treatment of the American colonies were being untrue to the ancient spirit of their own institutions. The slogan "Taxation without Representation Is Tyranny" was clearly founded on a British assumption. As James Otis put it in his pamphlet, *The Rights of the British Colonies* (1764), he believed "that this [British] constitution is the most free one, and by far the best, now existing on earth: that by this constitution, every man in the dominions is a free man: that no parts of His Majesty's dominions can be taxed without their consent: that every part has a right to be represented in the supreme or some subordinate legislature: that the refusal of this would seem to be a contradiction in practice to the theory of the constitution."

According to their own account, then, the Americans were to have forced on them the need to defend the ancient British tradition; to be truer to the spirit of that tradition than George III and Lord North and Townshend knew how to be. They were fighting not so much to establish new rights as to preserve old ones: "for the preservation of our liberties . . . in defence of the freedom that is our birthright, and which we ever enjoyed till the late violation of it" (Declaration of Causes of Taking up Arms, July 6, 1775). From the colonists' point of view, until 1776 it was Parliament that had been revolutionary, by exercising a power for which there was no warrant in English constitutional precedent. The ablest defender of the Revolution—in fact, the greatest political theorist of the American Revolution—was also the great theorist of British conservatism, Edmund Burke.

2. Second, the American Revolution was *not* the product of a nationalistic spirit. We had no Bismarck or Cavour or any nationalist philosophy. We were singularly free from most of the philosophical baggage of modern nationalism.

Perhaps never was a new nation created with less enthusiasm. To read the history of our Revolution is to discover that the United States was a kind of *pis aller*. This fact explains many of the difficulties encountered in conducting the Revolution and in framing a federal constitution. The original creation of a United States was the work of doubly reluctant men: men reluctant, both because of their local loyalties—to Virginia, Massachusetts, Rhode Island, and New York—and because of their imperial loyalty. The story of the "critical period" of American history, of the Articles of Confederation and the Constitution, tells of the gradual overcoming of this reluctance. It was overcome not by any widespread conversion to a nationalist theory—even the *Federalist* papers are conspicuously lacking in such a theory—but by gradual realization of the need for effective union.

In the period of the American Revolution we do discover a number of enthusiasms: for the safety and prosperity of Virginia or New York, for the cause of justice, for the rights of Englishmen. What is missing is anything that might be called widespread enthusiasm for the birth of a new nation: the United States of America. Until well into the nineteenth century, Jefferson—and he was not alone in this—was using the phrase "my country" to refer to his native state of Virginia.

3. Our Revolution was successful at the first try. This is equally true whether we consider it as a revolt against British rule or as a movement for republican federalism. There was no long-drawn-out agitation, no intellectual war of attrition, of the sort which breeds dogmas and intransigence. Thomas Paine's *Common Sense*, which is generally considered "the first important republican tract to be issued in America . . . the first to present cogent arguments for independence," did not appear until January 10, 1776. Down to within six months of the break, few would have considered independence; and even then the colonists had only quite specific complaints. There had been no considerable tradition in America either of revolt against British institutions or of republican theorizing.

The political objective of the Revolution, independence from British rule, was achieved by one relatively short continuous effort. More commonly in modern history (take, for example, the European revolutions of the nineteenth century) any particular revolt has been only one in a long series. Each episode, then, ends on a note of suspense which comes from the feeling that the story is "to be continued." Under those circumstances, challenges to constituted authority follow one another, accumulating their ideological baggage.

In France, for example, 1789 was followed by 1830 and 1848 and 1870; a similar list could be made for Italy, Germany, and perhaps Russia. Such repetition creates a

distinctive revolutionary tradition, with continued agitation keeping alive certain doctrines. Repeated efforts
provide the dogmatic raw material for a profusion of
later political parties, each of which rallies under the banner of one or another of the defeated revolutions or of a
revolution yet to be made. But, properly speaking, 1776
had no sequel, and needed none. The issue was separation, and separation was accomplished.

II. HOW WE HAVE BEEN LED TO IGNORE
THESE PECULIARITIES

The student who comes for the first time to the literature of our Revolution is liable to be disappointed by the
dull and legalistic flavor of what he has to read. Although
the American Revolution occurred in an age which
throughout Europe was laden with philosophic reflection
and important treatises, our Revolution was neither particularly rich nor particularly original in its intellectual
apparatus. The documents of that era, as Moses Coit
Tyler described them, are "a vast morass of technical
discussion, into which, perhaps, no living reader will ever
follow the writer, from which, in fact, the writer himself
never emerges alive."

Orators, textbook-writers, and other tradition-makers
have been hard put to it to find those ringing phrases, the
battle-cries and philosophical catchwords, which slip
smoothly off the tongue, remain fixed in the memory,
and uplift the soul. This helps explain why a few
phrases and documents have been overworked and why
even these have always been read only in part or out of

context. The first two paragraphs of the Declaration of Independence have been worn thin; few bother to read the remaining thirty. People have grasped at "life, liberty, and the pursuit of happiness," forgetting that it was two-thirds borrowed and, altogether, only part of a preamble. We have repeated that "all men are created equal," without daring to discover what it meant and without realizing that probably to none of the men who spoke it did it mean what we would like it to mean. Or we have exploited passages in the "speeches" of Patrick Henry, which were actually composed less by Henry than by his biographers.

The proper slogan of the Revolution—if, indeed, there was a slogan—was "No Taxation without Representation." Such words are far too polysyllabic, far too legalistic, to warm the popular heart. But if we compare them with the "Liberty, Equality, Fraternity" of the French Revolution and the "Peace, Bread, and Land," of the Russian, we have a clue to the peculiar spirit of the American Revolution. It is my view that the major issue of the American Revolution was the true constitution of the British Empire, which is a pretty technical legal problem. This notion is supported by Professor Charles H. McIlwain, who, in his admirable little book on the American Revolution, comes closer than any other recent historian to the spirit of our Revolutionary age.

In that age men were inclined to take their opponents at their word; the Revolutionary debate seems to have been carried on in the belief that men meant what they said. But in this age of Marx and Freud we have begun to take it for granted that, if people talk about one thing, they must be thinking about something else. Ideas are treated as the apparatus of an intellectual sleight-of-hand, by which the speaker diverts the audience's attention to an irrelevant subject while he does the real business unobserved. To study the Revolutionary debate is then to try to see (in the phrase of one historian) how "the colonists modified their theory to suit their needs." From such a point of view, there is perhaps never much political or legal thought worth talking about; to be realistic we should focus our discussion on hormones and statistics.

But such an approach would bleach away the peculiar tone of our history and empty our Revolution of its unique significance. Therefore, even at the risk of seeming naïve, I should like to consider the outlandish possibility that men like Jefferson and Adams all along meant what they were saying, that is, that the Revolution had something to do with the British constitution.

First, however, I should like briefly to describe the interpretation which in recent decades has had increasing vogue. That interpretation has taken two forms, both of which minimize the significance of the constitutional debate. Both views are instrumentalist and cosmopolitan in their emphasis: one starts from the history of ideas, and the other from economic history. The first of these is the point of view which was popularized by the late Carl Becker, who helped create the mold in which American accounts of the Revolution have been cast for the last several decades. According to this view, the colonists *began* their argument on a low legalistic level, finding it convenient to debate first within the framework of the imperial constitution and the common law; but they gradually and inevitably climbed the ladder of abstraction until, by mid-1776, they were thinking and talking in the arid heights of natural law.

"When the controversy with Great Britain began in 1764," Carl Becker writes in his influential book, *The Declaration of Independence*, "the preconceptions of the Natural Rights philosophy lay quiescent in colonial minds, ready to be drawn upon in case of need, but never yet having been called forth in the service of any concrete issue." Becker draws the lines from Locke and Newton forward to Franklin, Jefferson, and Adams, and he describes the several stages in the argument:

Thus step by step, from 1764 to 1776, the colonists modified their theory to suit their needs. They were not altogether unaware of the fact. . . . Profoundly convinced that they deserved to be free, Americans were primarily concerned with the moral or rational basis of their claims. . . . "If these now so considerable places are not represented, they ought to be." . . . But the "ought to be" is not ultimately to be found in positive law and custom. . . . Whenever men become sufficiently dissatisfied with what is, with the existing regime of positive law and custom, they will be found reaching out beyond it for the rational basis of what they conceive ought to be. This is what the Americans did in their controversy with Great Britain; and this rational basis they found in that underlying preconception which shaped the thought of their age—the idea of natural law and natural rights [(New York, 1933), pp. 133 f.].

By the time the Revolution became a fact, Americans were supposedly speaking the language of French philosophers. As they became more and more revolutionary, their argument, it is suggested, became less and less American.

A close reading of Becker reveals that he draws his evidence of the popularity of natural-law thinking more from English and French than from American sources. He does not offer us convincing examples of the adoption of Newtonian thinking into the writings of the American Revolutionary theorists. But, however this may be, any such interpretation is possible only if one projects back into the age of Jefferson a kind of skepticism about the common law and about the existence of rights themselves which was foreign to that age as a whole, and was especially antipathetic to our Revolutionary leaders.

The conventional account which we have been describing rests on an assumption that the colonists were engaged primarily—if not exclusively—in rationalizing their dissatisfactions. At the very least, it supposes a kind of intellectual mobility—near disingenuousness—which enabled the Americans to shift their ground to suit their needs. It takes for granted that colonial statements were mere polemics and therefore that the colonists could as readily abandon the legal for the philosophical level of argument as a hired counsel could alter his plea from guilty to not guilty. It overlooks certain obvious possibilities: that, all along, the colonists were saying what they really believed; that their loyalty to British institutions was itself a cause of the Revolution; and that therefore their enthusiasm for those institutions could not be put aside like a lawyer's brief.

The second form of the modern interpretation has been

rooted in a similarly cosmopolitan and instrumentalist frame of mind. This views our history not so much in the realm of general ideas as in the perspective of world economic development. Perhaps, it is suggested, the Revolution might better be seen as merely an episode in the growth of modern capitalism. The books of Charles A. Beard gave some support to this way of thinking. As Louis Hacker puts it in his *Triumph of American Capitalism:*

> The struggle was not over high-sounding political and constitutional concepts: over the power of taxation or even, in the final analysis, over natural rights. It was over colonial manufacturing, wild lands and furs, sugar, wine, tea, and currency, all of which meant, simply, the survival or collapse of English mercantile capitalism within the imperial-colonial framework of the mercantilist system [(New York, 1940), p. 161].

If the real motives were economic, the true purposes of the Revolutionaries lie hidden in financial archives, and what they said was actually not too important. The Revolutionary debate was only a frontier skirmish in the world-wide struggle for modern capitalism.

III. THE CONSERVATISM OF THE REVOLUTION

In order convincingly to refute either of these current views it would be necessary to retell the whole story of the Revolution. Obviously, this is not the place for such a narrative. My purpose here is rather to emphasize a certain aspect of the Revolution which in my opinion has not been given the emphasis it deserves. As new facts have been discovered and new interpretations manufactured, our historians have not readily added these new interpretations to the old, in order to produce a more complex and therefore perhaps a more valid explanation of a complex event. Rather they have been inclined to discard the wisdom of an older emphasis for that of a new. Hence it is that one of the more obvious aspects of the Revolution has been increasingly neglected.

The feature to which I want to direct your attention might be called the "conservatism" of the Revolution. If we understand this characteristic, we will begin to see the Revolution as an illustration of the remarkable continuity of American history. And we will also see how the attitude of our Revolutionary thinkers has engraved more deeply in our national consciousness a belief in the inevitability of our particular institutions, or, in a word, our sense of "givenness."

The character of our Revolution has nourished our assumption that whatever institutions we happened to have here (in this case the British constitution) had the self-evident validity of anything that is "normal." We have thus casually established the tradition that it is super-fluous to the American condition to produce elaborate treatises on political philosophy or to be explicit about political values and the theory of community.

I shall confine myself to two topics. First, the manifesto of the Revolution, namely, the Declaration of Independence; and, second, the man who has been generally considered the most outspoken and systematic political philosopher of the Revolution, Thomas Jefferson. Of course, I will not try to give a full account of either of them. I will attempt only to call your attention to a few facts which may not have been sufficiently emphasized and which are especially significant for our present purpose. Obviously, no one could contend that there is either in the man or in the document nothing of the cosmopolitan spirit, nothing of the world climate of opinion. My suggestion is simply that we do find another spirt of at least equal, and perhaps overshadowing, importance and that this spirit may actually be more characteristic of our Revolution.

First, then, for the Declaration of Independence. Its technical, legalistic, and conservative character, which I wish to emphasize, will appear at once by contrast with the comparable document of the French Revolution. Ours was concerned with a specific event, namely, the separation of these colonies from the mother-country. But the French produced a "Declaration of the Rights of *Man* and the Citizen." When De Tocqueville, in his *Ancien Régime* (Book I, chap. iii), sums up the spirit of the French Revolution, he is describing exactly what the American Revolution was not:

> The French Revolution acted, with regard to things of this world, precisely as religious revolutions have acted with regard to things of the other. It dealt with the citizen in the abstract, independent of particular social organizations, just as religions deal with mankind in general, independent of time and place. It inquired, not what were the particular rights of the French citizens, but what were the general rights and duties of mankind in reference to political concerns.
>
> It was by thus divesting itself of all that was peculiar to one race or time, and by reverting to natural principles of social order and government, that it became intelligible to all, and susceptible of simultaneous imitation in a hundred different places.

By seeming to tend rather to the regeneration of the human race than to the reform of France alone, it roused passions such as the most violent political revolutions had been incapable of awakening. It inspired proselytism, and gave birth to propagandism; and hence assumed that quasi religious character which so terrified those who saw it, or, rather, became a sort of new religion, imperfect, it is true, without God, worship, or future life, but still able, like Islamism, to cover the earth with its soldiers, its apostles, and its martyrs [trans. John Bonner (New York, 1856), pp. 26 f.].

In contrast to all this, our Declaration of Independence is essentially a list of specific historical instances. It is directed not to the regeneration but only to the "opinions" of mankind. It is closely tied to time and place; the special affection for "British brethren" is freely admitted; it is concerned with the duties of a particular king and certain of his subjects.

Even if we took only the first two paragraphs or preamble, which are the most general part of the document, and actually read them as a whole, we could make a good case for their being merely a succinct restatement of the Whig theory of the British revolution of 1688. Carl Becker himself could not overlook this fact. "In political theory and in political practice," he wrote parenthetically, "the American Revolution drew its inspiration from the parliamentary struggle of the seventeenth century. The philosophy of the Declaration was not taken from the French. It was not even new; but good old English doctrine newly formulated to meet a present emergency." To be understood, its words must be annotated by British history. This is among the facts which have led some historians (Guizot, for example) to go so far as to say that the English revolution succeeded twice, once in England and once in America.

The remaining three-quarters—the unread three-quarters—of the document is technical and legalistic. That is, of course, the main reason why it remains unread. For it is a bill of indictment against the king, written in the language of British constitutionalism. "The patient sufferance of these Colonies" is the point of departure. It deals with rights and franchises under British charters. It carefully recounts that the customary and traditional forms of protest, such as "repeated Petitions," have already been tried.

The more the Declaration is reread in context, the more plainly it appears a document of imperial legal relations rather than a piece of high-flown political philosophy. The desire to remain true to the principles of British constitutionalism up to the bitter end explains why, as has been often remarked, the document is directed against the king, despite the fact that the practical grievances were against Parliament; perhaps also why at this stage there is no longer an explicit appeal to the rights of Englishmen. Most of the document is a bald enumeration of George III's failures, excesses, and crimes in violation of the constitution and laws of Great Britain. One indictment after another makes sense only if one presupposes the framework of British constitutionalism. How else, for example, could one indict a king "for depriving us in many cases, of the benefits of Trial by Jury"?

We can learn a great deal about the context of our Revolutionary thought by examining Jefferson's own thinking down to the period of the Revolution. We need not stretch a point or give Jefferson a charismatic role, to say that the flavor of his thought is especially important for our purposes. He has been widely considered the leading political philosopher of the Revolution. Among other things, he was, of course, the principal author of the Declaration of Independence itself; and the Declaration has been taken to be the climax of the abstract philosophizing of the revolutionaries. Because he is supposed to be the avant-garde of revolutionary thought, evidence of conservatism and legalism in Jefferson's thought as a whole is especially significant.

We now are beginning to have a definitive edition of Jefferson's papers (edited by Julian P. Boyd and published by the Princeton University Press), which is one of the richest treasures ever amassed for the historian of a particular period. This helps us use Jefferson's thought as a touchstone. Neither in the letters which Jefferson wrote nor in those he received do we discover that he and his close associates—at least down to the date of the Revolution—showed any conspicuous interest in political theory. We look in vain for general reflections on the nature of government or constitutions. The manners of the day did require that a cultivated gentleman be acquainted with certain classics of political thought; yet we lack evidence that such works were read with more than a perfunctory interest. To be sure, when Jefferson prepares a list of worthy books for a young friend in 1771, he includes references to Montesquieu, Sidney, and Bolingbroke; but such references are rare. Even when he exchanges letters with Edmund Pendleton on the more general problems of institutions, he remains on the level of legality and policy, hardly touching political theory. Jefferson's papers for the Revolutionary period (read without the hindsight which has put the American and the French revolutions in the same era of world history) show little evidence that the American Revolution was a goad to higher levels of abstract thinking about society. We miss any such tendency in what Jefferson and his associates were reading or in what they were writing.

On the other hand, we find ample evidence that the locale of early Jeffersonian thought was distinctly *colonial*; we might even say *provincial*. And we begin to see some of the significance of that fact in marking the limits of political theorizing in America. By 1776, when the irreversible step of revolution was taken, the colonial period in the life of Jefferson and the other Revolutionary thinkers was technically at an end; but by then their minds had been congealed, their formal education completed, their social habits and the cast of their political thinking determined. The Virginia society of the pre-Revolutionary years had been decidedly derivative, not only in its culture, its furniture, its clothes, and its books, but in many of its ideas and—what is more to our purpose—in perhaps most of its institutions.

It is an important and little-noted fact that for many American thinkers of the period (including Jefferson himself) the cosmopolitan period in their thought did not begin until several years *after* their Revolution. Then, as representatives of the new nation, some of them were

to enter the labyrinth of European diplomacy. Much of
what we read of their experiences abroad even in this
later period would confirm our impression of their naïveté, their strangeness to the sophisticated Paris of Tal-
leyrand, the world of the *philosophes*. In Jefferson's particular case, the cosomopolitan period of his thought
probably did not begin much before his first trip abroad
as emissary to France in 1784.

When John Adams had gone, also to France, a few
years earlier on his first foreign mission, he thought himself fresh from an "American Wilderness." Still more
dramatic is the unhappy career of John Marshall, who
was an innocent abroad if there ever was one. The career
of Franklin, who was at least two generations older than
these Revolutionary leaders, is something of an exception; but even in his case much of his charm for the salons
of Paris consisted in his successful affectation of the character of a frontiersman.

The importance of this colonial framework in America, as I have already suggested, was to be enormous, not
only from the point of view of Revolutionary thought,
but in its long-run effect on the role of political theory in
American life. The legal institutions which Americans
considered their own and which they felt bound to master were largely borrowed. Jefferson and John Adams,
both lawyers by profession, like their English contemporaries, had extracted much of their legal knowledge out
of the crabbed pages of Coke's *Institutes*.

Now there were the elegant lectures of Sir William
Blackstone, published as the four-volume *Commentaries*

on the Laws of England, appearing between 1765 and 1769. It was this work of the ultra-conservative interpreter of English law that for many years remained the bible of American lawyers and, for several generations of them, virtually their whole bookish education. Blackstone's *Commentaries,* as Burke remarked in his Speech on Conciliation, had even by 1775 sold nearly as many copies in America as in England. American editions were numerous and popular; despite copious emendations and contradicting footnotes, Blackstone's original framework was faithfully preserved. Lincoln (as Carl Sandburg describes him), sitting barefoot on a woodpile in Illinois, fifty years later, reading the volumes of the conservative English lawyer—which he called the foundation of his own legal education—is a symbol of that continuity which has characterized our thinking about institutions. For our present purposes, the significant fact is that such a work as the *Commentaries* and the institutions which it expounded could continue to dominate the legal thinking of a people who were rebelling against the country of its origin.

During the very years when the Revolution was brewing, Jefferson was every day talking the language of the common law. We cannot but be impressed not only, as I have remarked, at the scarcity in the Jefferson papers for these years of anything that could be called fresh inquiry into the theory of government but also by the legalistic context of Jefferson's thought. We begin to see that the United States was being born in an atmosphere of legal rather than philosophical debate. Even apart from those technical legal materials with which Jefferson earned his living, his political pieces themselves possess a legal rather than a philosophical flavor.

A Summary View of the Rights of British America (July, 1774), which first brought Jefferson wide notice and which was largely responsible for his momentous choice on the committee to draft a declaration of independence, is less a piece of political theory than a closely reasoned legal document. He justifies the American position by appeal to the Saxon precedent: "No circumstance has occurred to distinguish materially the British from the Saxon emigration." It was from this parallel of the Americans with the Saxons, who also had once conquered a wilderness, that Jefferson draws several important legal consequences.

Jefferson's draft of the "new" Virginia Constitution of 1776 reveals a similar legalistic spirit: his Preamble comprised no premises of government in general, but only the same specific indictments of George III which were to be the substance of the Declaration of Independence. Jefferson actually describes the powers of the chief administrator as, with certain exceptions, "the powers formerly held by the king."

Jefferson's solid achievements in the period up to the Revolution were thus mainly works of legal draftsmanship. The reputation which he first obtained by his *Summary View*, he was to substantiate by other basic documents like the Virginia Constitution and by a host of complex public bills like those for dividing the county of Fincastle, for disestablishing the Church of England, for the naturalization of foreigners, and for the auditing of public accounts. Jefferson was equally at home in the intricacies of real-property law and in the problems of criminal jurisdiction. One of the many consequences of the neglect of American legal history has been our failure to recognize the importance of this legal element in our Revolutionary tradition. Jefferson's chef d'œuvre, a most impressive technical performance, was his series of Bills for Establishing Courts of Justice in Virginia. These bills, apparently drafted within about ten days in late 1776, show a professional virtuosity which any lawyer would envy.

The striking feature of these lawyerly accomplishments to those of us fed on clichés about the Age of Reason is how they live and move and have their being in the world of the common law, in the world of estates tail, bills in chancery, writs of supersedeas, etc., and not in the plastic universe of an eighteenth-century *philosophe*. Our evidence is doubly convincing, for the very reason that Jefferson was something of a reformer in legal matters. Yet even in his extensive projects of reform, he was eager to build on the foundation of the common law; for example, in his plan for the reform of the law of crimes and punishments. His tenacious conservatism appears in bold relief when we remind ourselves that Jefferson was a contemporary of Bentham, whose first important work, the *Fragment on Government*, also appeared in 1776.

But Jefferson did not found his reforms on any metaphysical calculus—rather on legal history and a continuity with the past. Even when he opposed feudal land tenures, he sought support from British sources. In the *Summary View* he had noted that feudal tenures were unknown to "our Saxon ancestors." "Has not every restitution of the antient Saxon laws had happy effects?" To have preserved the feudal tenures would actually have been, in Jefferson's words, "against the practice of our wise British ancestors. . . . Have not instances in which we have departed from this in Virginia been constantly condemned by the universal voice of our country?" (August 13, 1776; *Papers*, ed. Julian P. Boyd [Princeton, 1950], I, 492). Jefferson asked: "Is it not better now that we return at once into that happy system of our ancestors, the wisest and most perfect ever yet devised by the wit of man, as it stood before the 8th century?"

It is worth noting that Jefferson, who was to be the principal political philosopher of the Revolution, was given leadership in the important technical project of legal codification and reform in his native state of Virginia. Had he died at the end of 1776, he would probably have been remembered as a promising young lawyer of reformist bent, especially talented as a legal draftsman. In both houses of the Virginia legislature he had received the highest number of ballots in the election of members of the committee of legal revisers. The gist of the report of that committee (which included Edmund Pendleton, George Wythe, and George Mason, three of the ablest legal scholars on the continent, all active in the Revolution) is significant for our purposes. Jefferson himself recalled some years later that the commission had determined "not to meddle with the common law, i.e., the law preceding the existence of the statutes, further than to accommodate it to our new principles and circumstances."

Jefferson's philosophic concern with politics by the outbreak of the Revolution (actually only the end of his thirty-third year) was the enthusiasm of a reflective and progressive colonial lawyer for the traditional rights of Englishmen. To be sure, Jefferson did go further than some of his fellow-lawyers in his desire for legal reform— of feudal tenures, of entails, of the law of inheritance, of criminal law, and of established religion—yet even these projects were not, at least at that time, part of a coherent theory of society. They remained discrete reforms, "improvements" on the common law.

Jefferson's willingness to devote himself to purification of the common law must have rested on his faith in those ancient institutions and a desire to return to their essentials. This faith shines through those general maxims and mottoes about government which men took seriously in the eighteenth century and which often imply much more than they say. Jefferson's personal motto, "Rebellion to Tyrants Is Obedience to God," expresses pretty much the sum of his political theory—if, indeed, we should call it a "theory"—in this epoch. It was this motto (which Jefferson probably borrowed from Franklin, who offered it in 1776 for the Seal of the United States) that Jefferson himself proposed for Virginia and which he used on the seal for his own letters. But when we try to discover the meaning of the slogan to Jefferson, we find that it must be defined by reference less to any precise theology than to certain clear convictions about the British constitution. For who, after all, was a "tyrant"? None other than one who violated the sacred tenets of the ancient common law. Jefferson made his own view clear in the device which he suggested for the obverse of the United States seal: figures of "Hengist and Horsa, the Saxon chiefs from whom we claim the honor of being descended, and whose political principles and form of government we have assumed" (quoted by John Adams to Mrs. Adams, August 14, 1776; *Familiar Letters* [New York, 1875], p. 211).

In the Revolutionary period, when the temptations to be dogmatic were greatest, Jefferson did not succumb. The awareness of the peculiarity of America had not yet by any means led Jefferson to a rash desire to remake all society and institutions. What we actually discern is a growing tension between his feeling of the novelty of the American experience, on the one hand, and his feeling of belonging to ancient British institutions, on the other.

The tension was admirably expressed in Du Simitière's design for a coat of arms for Virginia. How large a hand Jefferson, who seems to have counseled Du Simitière, had in inventing the design is actually uncertain. But, regardless of authorship, the design eloquently portrays—indeed, almost caricatures—the current attitude. The indigenous glories of the New World were represented on the four quarters of the shield by a tobacco plant, two wheat sheafs, "a stalk of Indian corn full ripe," and "four fasces . . . alluding to the four gr[e]at rivers of Virginia." The background, the supporting and decorative elements—in fact, all parts of the arms that have any reference to institutions—emphasize the continuity of the British tradition. This was in August, 1776, after the date of the Declaration of Independence.

> Field a cross of St. george gules (as a remnant of the ancient coat of arms [showing] the origin of the Virginians to be English). . . . Supporters Dexter a figure dressed as in the time of Queen Elizabeth representing Sir Walter Rawleigh planting with his right hand the standard of liberty with the words MAGNA CHARTA written on it, with his left supporting the shield. Senester a Virginian rifle man of the present times compleatly ac-coutr[ed.]
> Crest. the crest of the antient arms of Virginia, the bust of a virgin naked and crowned with an antique crown. alluding to the Queen Elizabeth in whose reign the country was discover'd.
> Motto. "Rebellion to Tyrants is Obedience to God," or "Rex est qui regem non habet" [*Papers*, I, 510 ff.].

It would be possible to multiply examples of the importance of the continuing legal framework in the thought of other leaders of the Revolution. Few would be more interesting than John Adams, another of the authors of the Declaration of Independence. During the Revolutionary era, he elaborated a theory of the British Empire and developed in detail the notion of an unconstitutional act. His thought in this era has been characterized by Randolph G. Adams as that of a "Britannic Statesman."

IV. REVOLUTION WITHOUT DOGMA: A LEGACY
OF INSTITUTIONS

We begin to see how far we would be misled, were we to cast American events of this era in the mold of European history. The American Revolution was in a very special way conceived as both a vindication of the British

past and an affirmation of an American future. The British past was contained in ancient and living institutions
rather than in doctrines; and the American future was
never to be contained in a theory. The Revolution was
thus a prudential decision taken by men of principle rather than the affirmation of a theory. What British institutions meant did not need to be articulated; what America
might mean was still to be discovered. This continuity of
American history was to make a sense of "givenness"
easier to develop; for it was this continuity which had
made a new ideology of revolution seem unnecessary.

Perhaps the intellectual energy which American Revolutionaries economized because they were not obliged
to construct a whole theory of institutions was to
strengthen them for their encounter with nature and for
their solution of practical problems. The effort which
Jefferson, for example, did not care to spend on the theory of sovereignty he was to give freely to the revision of
the criminal law, the observation of the weather, the map-
ping of the continent, the collection of fossils, the study
of Indian languages, and the doubling of the national area.

The experience of our Revolution may suggest that the
sparseness of American political theory, which has sometimes been described as a refusal of American statesmen
to confront their basic philosophical problems, has been
due less to a conscious refusal than to a simple lack of
necessity. As the British colonists in America had forced
on them the need to create a nation, so they had forced
on them the need to be traditional and empirical in their
institutions. The Revolution, because it was conceived
as essentially affirming the British constitution, did not

95

create the kind of theoretical vacuum made by some other revolutions.

The colonial situation, it would seem, had provided a *ne plus ultra* beyond which political theorizing did not need to range. Even Jefferson, the greatest and most influential theorist of the Revolution, remained loath to trespass that boundary, except under pressure: the pressure of a need to create a new federal structure. Mainly in the realm of federalism were new expedients called for. And no part of our history is more familiar than the story of how the framers of the federal Constitution achieved a solution: by compromise on details rather than by agreement on a theory.

There is hardly better evidence of this fact than the character of *The Federalist* papers themselves. Nearly everything about them illustrates or even symbolizes the way of political thinking which I have tried to describe. *The Federalist or, The New Constitution* consists of essays written by Alexander Hamilton, James Madison, and John Jay and published one at a time in certain New York journals between late 1787 and early 1788. They had a simple practical purpose: to persuade the people of the state of New York to ratify the recently drawn federal Constitution. The eighty-five numbers were written, like any series of newspaper articles, to be read separately, each essay being a unit. Their object is summarized by Hamilton in No. 1:

I propose, in a series of papers, to discuss the following interesting particulars:—The utility of the UNION to your political prosperity—The insufficiency of the present Confederation to preserve that Union—The necessity of a government at least equally energetic with the one proposed, to the attainment of this object—The conformity of the proposed Constitution to the true principles of republican government—Its analogy to your own State constitution—and lastly, The additional security which its adoption will afford to the preservation of that species of government, to liberty, and to property.

If, indeed, *The Federalist* may be considered a treatise on political theory, it differs from other important works of the kind, by being an argument in favor of a particular written constitution. In this it is sharply distinguished from the writings of Plato, Aristotle, Hobbes, Locke, Rousseau, and J. S. Mill, which give us either systematic theories of the state or wide-ranging speculation. The organization of *The Federalist* papers is practical rather than systematic: they proceed from the actual dangers which confronted Americans to the weaknesses of the existing confederation and the specific advantages of the various provisions of the new constitution.

While the individual essays are full of wisdom, we must not forget, as Sir William Ashley reminds us, that "*The Federalist* has come to stand out more distinctly in the public view because of the oblivion that has befallen the torrent of other controversial writings of the same period." *The Federalist* essays are too often treated as if they comprised a single logical structure. They were a collaborative work mainly in the sense that their authors agreed on the importance of adopting the new constitution, not in the sense that the authors start from common and explicit philosophic premises. Hamilton, Madison, and Jay differed widely in personality and in philosophic position: individually they had even favored some other institutions than those embodied in the Constitution. But they had accepted the compromises and were convinced that what was being offered was far superior to what they already had. To read *The Federalist* is to discover the wisdom of Calhoun's observation that "this admirable federal constitution of ours . . . is superior to the wisdom of any or all of the men by whose agency it was made. The force of circumstances, and not foresight or wisdom, induced them to adopt many of its wisest provisions" (*Works*, ed. R. K. Cralle [New York, 1888], IV, 417).

The Revolution itself, as we have seen, had been a kind of affirmation of faith in ancient British institutions. In the greater part of the institutional life of the community the Revolution thus required no basic change. If any of this helps to illustrate or explain our characteristic lack of interest in political philosophy, it also helps to account for the value which we still attach to our inheritance from the British constitution: trial by jury, due process of law, representation before taxation, habeas corpus, freedom from attainder, independence of the judiciary, and the rights of free speech, free petition, and free assembly, as well as our narrow definition of treason and our antipathy to standing armies in peacetime. It also explains our continuing—sometimes bizarre, but usually fortunate—readiness to think of these traditional rights of Englishmen as if they were indigenous to our continent. In the proceedings of the San Francisco Vigilance Committee of 1851, we hear crude adventurers on the western frontier describing the technicalities of habeas corpus as if they were fruits of the American environment, as natural as human equality.

IV

THE CIVIL WAR AND THE
SPIRIT OF COMPROMISE

THE Civil War is the great trauma of our national life. It was probably the bloodiest civil war of the nineteenth century and perhaps even of all modern history. The cost in military lives alone was well over half a million. For us who boast that our political system is based on compromise, on the ability to organize varied regions and diverse institutions under a single federal union, it offers considerable embarrassment. At first sight it would seem the strongest possible contradiction of that continuity which I have been calling a characteristic of American political thought.

From any point of view it is one of the grimmest, most inexplicable, and most discouraging events of the modern era. But it has possessed a kind of morbid fascination for American historians. Like the woman who dwells on her operations, her symptoms, and the difficulties of her convalescence, we are apt to find that the details of our national misfortune are a good deal more interesting to ourselves than to others. Most listeners will be satisfied to know simply whether we survived. The South, which suffered most, has been the most voluble on the subject.

We have been so overwhelmed by the uniqueness of

the Civil War in our history that we have readily over-looked some of the ways in which it illustrates persistent characteristics of our political thinking. In this chapter I shall try to show how the circumstances of the struggle circumscribed the Civil War debate and prevented it from becoming a free-for-all among political theorists. It was even to reinforce our sense of the continuity of our history.

Fortunately, it will not be necessary for my purpose to go into the question of the "causes" of the war, which is one of the most debated matters in our history. It is sufficient here to assume that there were a number of deeper "causes" and that these, taken together with many casual facts, precipitated the war. The casual factors which must not be forgotten were the sort of thing enumerated by J. G. Randall as "the despairing plunge, the unmotivated drift, the intruding dilemma, the blasted hope, the self-fulfilling prediction, the push-over, the twisted argument, the frustrated leader, the advocate of rule or ruin, and the reform-your-neighbor prophet." I shall direct your attention not so much to the causes of the conflict as to the framework of the debate.

Two obvious features of the American Civil War were to affect the mood of the discussion. They distinguish our Civil War from most other conflicts that go under that name in the nineteenth and twentieth centuries. From these we can derive much of the significance of the event for the place of theory in American political life:

1. The Civil War was a *sectional* conflict: a struggle between two geographically separate regions; in the ver-

nacular, it was a war between "the North" and "the South."

2. The Civil War was a *federal* conflict: just as the American Revolution was a struggle within a colonial framework, so the Civil War was a struggle within a well-established, working federal scheme.

If these two points are obvious to the point of platitude, their implications are perhaps somewhat less obvious and are of great significance for our way of political thought. I shall deal with them in turn.

I. SECTIONALISM: SOCIOLOGY STANDS IN FOR POLITICAL THEORY

One of the main questions which disturbed people at the time of the formation of the federal Union was whether a republican government could long endure, or even exist, over an extensive and varied continent. "It is natural for a republic," Montesquieu had written in a familiar passage in his *Spirit of Laws* (Book VIII, sec. 16) in 1748, "to have only a small territory; otherwise it cannot long subsist. . . . In a small one, the interest of the public is more obvious, better understood, and more within the reach of every citizen."

The authors of *The Federalist* later argued that precisely the contrary of this was true; that the extent and variety of the American union would be its safeguard against the evils of "faction." "Extend the sphere," Madison wrote in the famous No. 10, "and you take in a greater variety of parties and interests; you make it less probable that a majority of the whole will have a common motive to invade the rights of other citizens; or if such a common motive exists, it will be more difficult for all who feel it to discover their own strength, and to act in unison with each other." Jefferson emphatically agreed (at least after the defeat of his opponents, the Federalists): "Had our territory been even a third only of what it is, we were gone." Whether the Civil War was actually proof or disproof of the optimistic American position, whether the rise of mass communications does not radically alter the premises—these are questions that need not concern us here.

What we need to consider is a much more limited question. How has the remarkable extent and variety of the United States been related to the place of theory in our political life? For this question the Civil War is of the greatest interest.

Whatever else one may say of the other "causes" of the Civil War, if it had not been for the great differences of soil, climate, and topography and what those differences had come to mean in institutions, the Civil War would hardly have been conceivable. We know, recalling the Hartford Convention of 1814, that the states'-rights tradition—at least until the issues of tariff and slavery came to the fore—was as strong in New England as in the South. We know, on the other hand, that the sentimental and intellectual attachment to the Constitution even until the very verge of the Civil War was at least as strong in the South as in New England.

The sectional character of the Civil War is as plain a feature of our history as the Mississippi River is of our

geography. Yet its importance for the mode of our political thought has not been sufficiently noted. The fact
that the conflict was along sectional lines, that each side
purported to be fighting in defense of its institutions and
way of life, made any elaborate philosophizing on the
subject seem superfluous. The Civil War will thus provide an admirable illustration of our tendency to make
sociology do for political theory, to merge the descriptive and the normative, to draw the "ought" out of the
"is." Or, in a word, to confirm our belief in "givenness."

Neither North nor South was pursuing a new vision
of society. Much of the polemical effort on either side
took the form of describing its own institutions and those
of its enemy. The upshot was both a stimulus to sociology and an incentive to make facts serve a normative
purpose. Seldom has there been a stronger practical motive to lay bare the relationship among apparently diverse
facts about a society: among the political system, economic structure, and labor practices of a region and its
religion, morals, art, literature, and culture as a whole.
The Mason and Dixon Line was thus a symbol not only
of the regional nature of the conflict but also of the fact
that, theoretically speaking, the conflict was to be waged
on an empirical rather than a metaphysical battlefield.

Too little attention has been given to the ways in
which the attempt to defend or attack sectional interests
(and especially the institution of slavery) stimulated the
growth of sociology as a separate social science. In the
nineteenth century in England, France, and Germany social conflict stimulated economic, legal, and political the-

ory. Through a series of local accidents in the United States, intellectual energies were canalized into sociology, the quest for interrelations among facts about institutions.

American sociology dates from before the Civil War: actually from the very period in which the ramifications of slavery and of the "peculiar" institutions of each of the two sections of the country were being explored. Our intellectual historians have been too ready to father American sociology upon Charles Darwin, whose *Origin of Species* appeared in 1859, and upon his contemporary, Herbert Spencer. They generally date the origins of American sociology from Lewis H. Morgan, Lester F. Ward, Charles H. Cooley, William Graham Sumner, and Thorstein Veblen, all of whom flourished after our Civil War. But we should look to an earlier period, when the debate over slavery had produced a characteristically American sociology.

A good deal of the sociological literature of the 1850's was, of course, crudely apologetic or polemical—but by no means all of it. At least one serious attempt at *The Science of Society*, by Stephen Pearl Andrews (whose personal starting point was the institution of slavery) long antedated Sumner's work of the same title. Perhaps never before in American history had there been such enthusiasm for describing cultures as wholes, for seeing interrelations. Nor had there ever been such a relentless determination to make the facts—to torture them, if necessary, in order to make them—"speak for themselves." That many of the writers set out from the question of slavery did not prevent their works from having some general significance in the evolution of American sociology. Quite the contrary. The peculiar fact that slavery had a regional distribution on the American continent made it possible to set up competing concepts of culture, based on much the same kind of data which would interest a modern sociologist.

Among the most important of these scholars was George Frederick Holmes, for forty years professor of "historical science" and literature at the University of Virginia. Holmes was, of course, an apologist for slavery. But he was at the same time a respectable sociologist, well thought of by Auguste Comte himself, whose writings he was among the first to introduce into this country. But he was only one of several, for men like Henry Hughes of Mississippi and George Fitzhugh of Virginia also used the word "sociology." Though Fitzhugh gave the word his own special meaning, he, like the others, wrote treatises on the subject and was not without understanding of what such a science might mean.

On the northern side there was the erratic Stephen Pearl Andrews of New York. He showed that the new sociology was not wholly partisan when he proposed to Holmes and Andrews in 1855 that they collaborate on a definitive sociological work which might be "broad enough to cover North and South, to neutralize factious demagoguism against the institutions of one section, to enlighten and liberalize all sections, to quicken lagging conservatism of the South into reform in its own way, and adapted to its own wants, and to give the reformers of the North quite enough to attend to at home." Andrews expressed the ostensible purpose of all these writers when he said he was mainly interested in inquiring into "the true or requisite moral and social *habitat* of the spiritual animal called man."

These pioneer sociologists illustrate a significant general characteristic of American thought in the era of our Civil War, a characteristic which reflected the persistent peculiarities of American history and geography. Sociology was actually playing the role of political theory. Instead of speculating about The Good State, thinkers worked at the anatomy of institutions. Scholars like Holmes and Andrews were by no means unique. We can find many other examples of sociological writing in the main current of the pre–Civil War argument. Such men seemed to express the mode in which many people were thinking. For this was a *sectional* conflict. The contention on both sides that slavery or free labor was intimately bound up with all a community's values had stimulated an interest in the culture of each section as a whole.

Every statistical detail became a clue to a way of life. "Givenness" was here expressed in the assumption that life as it was in America—whether in the North or in the South—gave the outlines of life as it ought to be, that values were implicit in experience. The tradition of seeking norms, not in theological or philosophical speculation, but in the texture of American life, was thus enriched and reinforced by the form of our Civil War controversy.

II. FACTS SPEAK FOR THEMSELVES

The pressures in this direction will be apparent if we start with the less familiar of the two arguments, that on the side of the South. From the nature of the southern case, it was hard to find any simplistic position similar to that of the abolitionists in the North. To be sure, there were a few, especially among the clergy, who argued that slavery was a commandment of God and who tried to make an absolute of it. But such a position was, for obvious reasons, difficult to maintain and did not excite much fervor.

The more tenable southern position, which was widely elaborated by respectable scholars, was of a different character. This is what I characterize as the "sociological" argument. It tended to sidestep the moral issue, to avoid the appeal to absolutes—or even in some cases to admit that slavery might be a moral evil. "It is said," Dew admitted, "slavery is wrong, in the *abstract* at least, and contrary to the spirit of Christianity. To this we answer as before, that any question must be determined by its circumstances, and if, as really is the case, we cannot get rid of slavery without producing a greater injury to both the masters and slaves, there is no rule of conscience or revealed law of God which *can* condemn us" (*Essay on Slavery* [2d ed.; Richmond, Va., 1849], p. 93).

Men like Thomas Dew asked that you take a look at southern society as a whole. They tried to describe that society in detail and then assumed that mere inspection would reveal the superiority of the southern social system. They were assuming that the values would emerge from the facts. They were presupposing the "givenness" of values. Such an argument would not have been persuasive, had it not been: first, that they were discussing "slavery," an institution which already existed and could be observed in operation; and, second, that the conflict in which they were engaged was sectional, so that a description of the actual superiorities of their section would seem to clinch the case.

The keynote of this argument was struck by George Fitzhugh, in the opening paragraph of his *Sociology for the South*. "Society has been so quiet and contented in the South," he wrote, "—it has suffered so little from crime or extreme poverty, that its attention has not been awakened to the revolutionary tumults, uproar, mendicity and crime of free society. Few are aware of the blessings they enjoy, or of the evils from which they are exempt." In a variety of ways the most respectable intellectuals in the South tried to make the facts speak for themselves. They tried to show how a fair and complete view of southern culture and the southern economy would automatically answer the question at issue. Their facts were intricate, their lines of causation devious and sometimes tenuous. But their preoccupation was with the facts: the connection between slavery and everything else that went on in the South; the relation of labor systems to the accumulation of capital, to leisure, religion, literature, science, and the position of women.

We could hardly make a greater mistake than to dismiss these thinkers as mere partisans and crackpots.

Among them, as Harvey Wish has shown, were men of vigor, individuality, and learning, who had a great deal to say that was worth listening to, about both southern and northern institutions.

The ablest, the most original, and perhaps the most widely read of these was Fitzhugh himself. In his two books, *Sociology for the South* and *Cannibals All*, he compared slave society as a whole with free society as a whole. His thesis was that, while slave society was peaceable and exempt from the major "social afflictions," free society was a failure. For, he said, in all societies the ownership of man by man must exist in some form or other, and the form which free societies had given to such ownership was hypocritical, unproductive, and demoralizing. In a so-called "free society," Fitzhugh argued, masters were irresponsible, women debased, and laborers indolent. All workers were "slaves without masters." A "free" man had no owner but the state, and the state was the least humane of all masters. He describes the troubles of the "free" laborer in a competitive society and the sufferings of women and children in factories. These he contrasts with the thrift and humanity of the slave system.

In a vein reminiscent of R. H. Tawney's *Acquisitive Society* (a socialist critique of twentieth-century capitalism), Fitzhugh mocks the "morality" of a competitive system:

> In free society none but the selfish virtues are in repute, because none other help a man in the race of competition. In such society virtue loses all her loveliness, because of her selfish aims.

Good men and bad men have the same end in view: self-promotion and self-elevation. The good man is prudent, cautious, and cunning of fence; he knows well, the arts (the virtues, if you please) which enable him to advance his fortunes at the expense of those with whom he deals; he does not "cut too deep"; he does not cheat and swindle, he only makes good bargains and excellent profits. He gets more subjects by this course; everybody comes to him to be bled. He bides his time; takes advantage of the follies, the improvidence and vices of others, and makes his fortune out of the follies and weaknesses of his fellow-men. The bad man is rash, hasty, unskilful and impolitic. He is equally selfish, but not half so prudent and cunning. Selfishness is almost the only motive of human conduct in free society, where every man is taught that it is his first duty to change and better his pecuniary situation [*Sociology for the South* (Richmond, Va., 1854), pp. 24 f.].

No historian of the period could deny that Fitzhugh had put his finger on a real weakness of northern society in the 1850's.

Another of the leading southern apologists for slavery was Thomas Dew, president of William and Mary College after 1836. He, too, set his defense in a sociological frame. While not going so far as Chancellor Harper, who called slavery "the sole cause" of civilization, Dew showed how, historically, the rise of slavery had been connected with the mitigation of the evils of war, emergence from a hunting to an agricultural economy, and improvement in the position of women. Dew was actually a pioneer in the teaching of social sciences in the United States. His *Digest of the Laws, Customs, Manners, and Institutions of the Ancient and Modern Nations* (1853) showed an extraordinary breadth of learning and an impressive ability to go beyond the conventional boundaries of political history.

Statistics were put into the service of sociology by James D. B. de Bow, publisher of one of the most influential southern reviews. He had been superintendent of the United States census of 1850, was by profession a statistician, and employed a heavy artillery of facts and figures to prove such propositions as Fitzhugh's that "the wealth of the South is permanent and real, that of the North fugitive and fictitious." "Your wealth is cosmopolitan," Fitzhugh warned New England from the pages of *De Bow's Review* (XXIII [1857], 587), "Your poverty indigenous!"

On the northern side it was perhaps easier to be absolutist and abstract: to argue that slavery was a moral evil and leave it at that. This was, of course, the abolitionist position of men like Wendell Phillips and William Lloyd Garrison. Nowadays historians are inclined to minimize the role of the abolitionists, whether as an expression of public opinion or as an influence in northern politics.

However effective the abolitionists may have been as agitators who kept the fires of controversy burning, sabotaged efforts at compromise, and fed the spirit of intransigence, the politically effective northern opposition to slavery was actually of a different character. It was, in fact, based less on love for the Negro than on concern for the white workingman; less on a feeling for the present sufferings of the slave than on a fear for the future plight of the white man if everywhere in the Union he should have to compete with the Negro. The fear of the

North was in this sense based less on the evil than on the contagion of slavery: that it disintegrated the community, depressed the standard of living, and degraded everyone.

This involved a direct refutation of the southern sociological argument. Northerners contended that where slavery flourished the community declined, and where freedom flourished the community prospered. The converse of the argument was also, of course, readily assumed. Thus to prove the economic and social decline of the South would prove the evil of slavery; and the prosperity of the North would prove the good of free labor. Even abolitionists were not beyond using this line of reasoning. Wendell Phillips, speaking at New Haven in 1855, replied to Fitzhugh's defense of slavery:

> An hour spent upon either of the two hills that guard your city, the East and West Rock, looking down thence upon your population, its Christianity, its churches, upon every man therein the founder of his own fortunes, the head of his family household, training it up by the Bible, upon an industry that uses every drop of water ten times over before it lets it fall into the sea, upon an education that lifts up not only your own State, but spreads and runs through the nation—one hour, if spent there, tells us that he who can look at all this, and say it has failed, must look elsewhere than upon this earth for success [*New Haven Weekly Palladium*, March 31, 1855; quoted in Harvey Wish, *Fitzhugh* (Baton Rouge, 1943), p. 139].

Similarly, Seward in his famous "Irrepressible Conflict" speech at Rochester on October 25, 1858, observed that "the great melioration of human society which modern times exhibit, is mainly due to the incomplete substitution of the system of voluntary labor for the old one of servile labor." From slavery, he said, came "poverty, imbecility, and anarchy," while to the system of free labor could be ascribed "the strength, wealth, greatness, intelligence, and freedom, which the whole American people now enjoy."

There was perhaps no better exponent of this position than Lincoln himself. As we all know, Lincoln on more than one occasion declared himself to be no abolitionist. The emancipation of slaves was to be forced on him as a wartime military necessity, and he did what he could to postpone and avoid it. He seems to have had very little enthusiasm to make Virginia or South Carolina a free state but was quite determined that Illinois should *not* become a slave state. The same concern governed his attitude to the territories. As he said at Peoria in 1854, "The whole nation is interested that the best use shall be made of these Territories. We want them for homes of free white people. This they cannot be, to any considerable extent, if slavery shall be planted within them." "If free negroes should be made *things,* how long, think you," he is reported to have asked at Bloomington in May, 1856, "before they will begin to make *things* out of poor white men?" The familiar aphorism that the Union could not long exist half-slave and half-free, in his speech at Springfield on June 16, 1858, was no trick of rhetoric. It was another way of saying that, if slavery continued to exist anywhere in the Union, free northern workmen would before long find themselves, like the poor southern whites, competing with the labor of Negroes. In every one of his recorded speeches from 1854 until his election to the presidency, as Richard Hofstadter has observed, Lincoln used this argument: opposing the extension of slavery because of its effect on *white* workingmen.

The striking feature of this argument is its complexity and indirectness, compared with the crusading shibboleths of men like Garrison and Weld, from which sensible northerners dissociated themselves. Jefferson, in his *Notes on Virginia*, had set a precedent for this way of thinking. His criticism of slavery was sociological: he had observed its effect on the manners and morals of white people—and especially of children. He had noted how the demoralizing influence was intensified by the warm climate, where "no man will labor for himself who can make another labor for him." Like the Jeffersonian, the Lincolnian position assumed that one knew and could take for granted the sort of life desirable for the white community. It made no sense unless one could establish the numerous factual links between slavery for the black man and evils for the white man, or for the community as a whole. This committed the question, not to the student of ethics or political philosophy, but to the sociologist, the statistician, the master of facts.

The way such factual links were forged can be observed in Hinton R. Helper's *Impending Crisis of the South*, perhaps the most successful book of its kind written in support of the northern position. First published in 1857, it was later subsidized by the Republican party, reissued in abridged form, and circulated by the thousands. Democratic editorial writers blamed John Brown's Raid in large part on works like Helper's. But if we look at the book today, we can see that, however inflammatory its effect, it was pretty devious and factual in its argument.

Taking for his motto a passage from Agassiz on the value of "comparisons" for enabling one to rise from particular facts to the "general features of things," Helper sets out by disavowing any intention to produce either a philosophical disquisition or a treatise on ethics. "Self-evident truths," he asserts, "require no argumentative demonstration."

What we mean to do is simply this: to take a survey of the relative position and importance of the several states of this confederacy, from the adoption of the national compact; and when, of two sections of the country starting under the same auspices, and with equal natural advantages, we find the one rising to a degree of almost unexampled power and eminence, and the other sinking into a state of comparative imbecility and obscurity, it is our determination to trace out the causes which have led to the elevation of the former, and the depression of the latter, and to use our most earnest and honest endeavors to utterly extirpate whatever opposes the progress and prosperity of any portion of the Union [*Impending Crisis* (New York, 1860), p. 7].

By copious statistics Helper proceeds to show that, while the free states had lagged far behind the slave states at the time of the formation of the Union, by mid-century the position was reversed. New York, for example, possessed only half the population of Virginia in 1790, but twice the population of Virginia in 1850. The exports of New York were originally below those of Virginia, but by 1850 had come to exceed Virginia's forty fold. And so on. Massachusetts is set against North Carolina, Pennsylvania against South Carolina.

Helper argues at length that slavery has depressed all real-estate values in the South. Therefore, to abolish slavery will indirectly compensate slaveowners for the value of the slaves. By nearly fifty statistical tables Helper demonstrates that in the North population, agriculture, commerce, and education increase, circulation of Bibles and newspapers is vast, science and literature flourish, and even the hogs grow ever larger, while in the South everything deteriorates. Whatever one may think of the causal chain by which Helper tries to link the institution of slavery with these other facts, there is no denying that he offers an impressive statistical apparatus. Even his critics must admit that he has made an effort toward descriptive sociology, toward putting together a picture of the large differences between the cultures and economies of two regions. The spirit of this approach to political issues is well summarized when Helper says: "Slavery has polluted and impoverished your lands; freedom will restore them to their virgin purity, and add from twenty to thirty dollars to the value of every acre."

This attempt at a sociological approach—at describing the totality of the southern or the northern culture—was, of course, based upon the assumption that the good and the bad would emerge from the facts themselves. The numerous travelers, southerners in the North or northerners in the South, wrote their books on this assumption. Among the more important of these was Frederick L. Olmsted, whose writings today remain of some value. His approach was less statistical than reportorial, but still conspicuously sociological. As Olmsted explained in the

Preface to his *Journey in the Back Country*, he was looking for "the matter of fact of the condition of the people, especially the white people, living under a great variety of circumstances where slavery is not prohibited." He did what the modern sociologist might have called "field work," as he traveled through the South, observed (not without bias) the way of life, the minutiae of diet, manners, customs, and morals, trying to show the ramifications of slavery and its effects on the white population and on the society as a whole.

The most popular book of the controversy was, of course, no explicitly sociological tract but a kind of sociological novel, *Uncle Tom's Cabin*. No work could better illustrate the tendency we are describing—to let the "facts" speak for themselves. It was hardly necessary for Mrs. Stowe to elaborate her intention that the novel should depict a social system as a whole and not a few extreme examples. But she actually published a "Key" to her book to prove that all the incidents she recounted were simply illustrative.

Perhaps the least characteristic (if most familiar) product of the Civil War controversy was the flood of abolitionist literature. It is easy to read because it is concrete and usually lurid. Much of it falls into that class of "atrocity" journalism which has become familiar enough. Its significance for our present argument is only incidental. But we should not fail to note that (*a*) like all atrocity literature, the abolitionist works presupposed agreement on values; and (*b*) their force depended on the claim to be factual.

In such forms as these the sectional character of the controversy had brought champions on both sides to cast their defense and their attack. They were unwittingly led to speak the language of facts, of statistics; to talk of the "success" or "failure" of cultures. It seemed easier and more relevant to describe northern or southern "conditions" as a whole than to argue over the criteria by which societies should be judged. If the struggle was, indeed, between "the North" and "the South," one could understand it best by simply examining those entities. What was to be characteristic of our history was not simply the circumstances which framed a sectional civil war over certain issues, but also how that way of framing issues flavored our political thought. Thus the debate, though sometimes passionate, was still on the whole focused on the "facts" of the two regions. Both sides appeared to believe that such data would answer any questions about the good society.

III. THE SECOND WAR OF INDEPENDENCE

FEDERALISM LIMITS THE DEBATE

In the first part of this chapter I described some of the ways in which the *sectional* character of the American Civil War fenced in our political speculation, making sociology do for political theory, and hence confirming our tendencies toward belief in the "givenness" of our values. Now I shall turn to a second distinguishing feature of our Civil War: the simple fact that it was a *federal* conflict. This second peculiarity also may help explain why our political theorizing in that age did not range so widely as it has in many of the civil conflicts of modern European history.

As the American Revolution had been a struggle within a long-established colonial framework, so the Civil War was a struggle within a working federal system. The two events were to have analogous consequences in hedging in our political reflection, and in identifying the special institutions of this country with the normal conditions of life on this continent. Whatever theoretical debate went on, with few exceptions, was concerned not with the nature of governments but rather with the nature of this particular government.

That the Civil War was a federal conflict, like the colonial character of our Revolution, seems, perhaps, too obvious to require elaboration. But some of our ablest recent historians have given currency to an emphasis which has tended to obscure, or even to displace, the obvious.

In their brilliant *Rise of American Civilization*, Charles A. and Mary R. Beard christened the Civil War "The Second American Revolution." The phrase and the idea have had wide appeal. It has suited our current attitudes to suspect that the actual subject of debate was not the real cause of the conflict. The battle itself, supposedly, was but a symptom of deeper forces: "the social cataclysm in which the capitalists, laborers, and farmers of the North and West drove from power in the national government the planting aristocracy of the South . . . the social revolution was the essential, portentous outcome." Without denying that such a social revolution was taking place, we can recall that there was another side to the conflict. If we turn our attention from inevitable forces to human debate, we must look primarily at a different aspect of the struggle. This is only appropriate, since we are concerned with the place of theory in our conscious political life.

The name "The Second American Revolution" given by the Beards and their disciples, is misleading. They (and others who find the center of change in economic events) would thus emphasize the *dis*continuity of our history: the Civil War as a hiatus in our development, a gulf between an agricultural-commercial and an industrial society. But to those students who, like me, are impressed by the extraordinary continuity of our history, such an emphasis seems distortion. As we all know, the great economic developments are slow, evolutionary, and sometimes imperceptible; their triumphs are not self-announced in manifestoes. The Industrial Revolution was a matter of centuries, and the kind of revolution to which the Beards refer must also have been a matter of decades.

But *political* history (such events as go by the name of "revolution" and "civil war") has the abruptness of mutation. It is therefore in this area that it would be especially significant to note that what is called a great gulf in our history may not be so great as has been supposed. One of the remarkable characteristics of our Civil War, as contrasted with civil wars of recent European history (excepting possibly the English Civil War), is that ours did *not* significantly interrupt the continuity of our thinking about institutions.

From the point of view of political and constitutional thought, we might do better to call our Civil War "The Second War of Independence." I have already mentioned Guizot's remark that the English Revolution succeeded twice, once in England in the seventeenth century and a second time in America in the eighteenth. We might go further and say that, from the point of view of constitutional law and political theory, the Revolution occurred a third time, namely, in the middle of the nineteenth century. For the relation of the ancient rights of Englishmen to federalism, which was only partly redefined in the course of the American Revolution, was more extensively explored and settled during the Civil War.

That continuity of our political thought which, as we have seen, had been expressed in the legalistic character of the American Revolutionary debate was also expressed later in much of the argument over the Civil War. There is even less evidence here for the pattern which Carl Becker saw in the Revolution. The main current did not seem to rise above the "provincial" level of constitutionalism to the more "cosmopolitan" atmosphere of natural law. Indeed, we find something of the opposite of what Becker remarks as the increasing abstractness of Revolutionary debate. In the South at least, as the crisis proceeded the debate seemed to become more and more legalistic, reaching its climax actually after the war was over. The legal debate never rose to the realm of natural law, not even to the extent found in the American Revolution.

The North and the South each considered that it was fighting primarily for its legal rights under the sacred federal Constitution. A man like Thoreau probably stood only for himself and a few fire-eating abolitionists. On neither side do we hear much of the sort of argument familiar in European civil wars: that the existing federal constitution was bad and ought to be changed, and that was what one should fight for. On the contrary, each side purported to represent the authentic original doctrine, to be *defending* the Constitution.

Calhoun, who was by far the most profound of the southern writers on the subject, shows this peculiarity. His major theoretical work, not published until after his death in 1850, consists of two parts: "A Disquisition on Government" and "A Discourse on the Constitution and Government of the United States." It is on these that his growing reputation as a political philosopher largely depends. These works taken together (as Calhoun intended that they should be) admirably illustrate the point of view I have been describing.

The "Disquisition," an essay of about a hundred pages, though starting from some general principles of psychology and political theory, is primarily a defense of Calhoun's principle of the "concurrent majority" and an exposition of his objections to governments based on the "numerical majority." In a closely reasoned argument, Calhoun points out the dangers of uncontrolled majority rule. The only safeguard, he insists, is a system of constitutionalism which will allow each separate interest a veto on all legislation to which it objects. Such a system, he urges, results in moderation and compromise and still can leave government strong enough to combat enemies from without. He supports his argument by the experience of Rome, Poland, and Great Britain.

"A Discourse on the Constitution and Government of the United States," a work about three times the length of the "Disquisition," is the sequel. In it Calhoun tries to show that "it was the object of the framers of the constitution, in organizing the government, to give to the two elements [the states as units and the voting population], of which it is composed, separate, but concurrent action; and, consequently, a veto on each other, whenever the organization of the department, or the nature of the power would admit: and when this could not be done, so to blend the two, as to make as near an approach to it, in effect, as possible. It is, also, apparent, that the government, regarded apart from the constitution, is the government of the concurrent, and not of the numerical majority" (*Works*, I, 181).

By reference to the proceedings of the Philadelphia convention and of the ratifying conventions, Calhoun demonstrates that, through a happy coincidence, the true and original conception of the federal Constitution was actually nothing but a design for the attainment of his ideal government. The departure from his ideal, the gradual growth of a consolidated national government, and the development of means by which one section could dominate another were all to be explained as departures from the true intent of the Framers.

To the one, or to the other,—to monarchy, or disunion it must come, if not prevented by strenuous and timely efforts. And this brings up the question,—How it is to be prevented? How can these sad alternatives be averted? For this purpose, it is indispensable that the government of the United States should be restored to its federal character. Nothing short of a perfect restoration, as it came from the hands of its framers, can avert them [*Works*, I, 381].

This restoration was to be effected by getting rid of certain perversions which had been introduced after the adoption of the Constitution. Calhoun urges, for example, the repeal of Section 25 of the Judiciary Act of 1789, and of the Act of 1833; "the repeal of all acts by which the money power is carried beyond its constitutional limits"; the confining of the president to those powers expressly conferred on him by the Constitution and by acts of Congress; the return in practice to the original way of electing the president and vice-president.

Such means as these—together with a few reforms like the introduction of a plural executive—would, in Calhoun's phrase, "complete the work of restoration." We are never allowed to forget that what Calhoun aims at is not revolution but *restoration*.

IV. A CONFLICT OF ORTHODOXIES

Here, once again, was a competition between constitutional orthodoxies. As often in American history, a great political conflict was taking the form not of a struggle between essentially different political theories but between differences of constitutional emphasis. There was a striking, if obvious, parallel to the epoch of the

Revolution. But the South was now even more conservative than the Revolutionaries had been. It found no reason to issue a Declaration of Independence. The colonists had set themselves up as defenders of the British constitution and contended that it was not they but the parliament who were actually the revolutionaries. So now, champions of the South could—and did—argue that it was not they, but the northerners, who were, properly speaking, the revolutionaries. Each accused the other of seeking to overthrow the established doctrine of the federal Constitution, the ideas of the Founding Fathers.

The Civil War secessionist argument—like that of the Revolution—could be carried on in such a conservative vocabulary because both events were, theoretically speaking, only surface breaches in a firm federal framework. Because of this, they both implied, win or lose, the continued acceptance of the existing structure of local government. Thus in the Civil War southern partisans, like the Americans in the Revolution, could continue to profess loyalty to the theory of the Union. As a New Yorker championing the Southern cause declared in 1860:

The South views the matter in the spirit of Patrick Henry. "The object is now, indeed, small, but the shadow is large enough to darken all this fair land." They can have no faith in men who profess what they think a great moral principle, and deny that they intend to act upon it. It was the principle of taxation without representation that the colonies resisted, and it is the principle of the "irrepressible conflict," based avowedly on a "higher law," that the South resists. She is now in the position of the Colonies eighty-four years ago, and is adopting the same measures that they adopted. . . . A prompt retreat from this dangerous agitation within the shadow of the Constitution, is the

only means of realizing the rich future, which will be the reward
only of harmony, good faith, and loyalty to the Constitution
[Thomas P. Kettell, *Southern Wealth and Northern Profits*
(New York, 1860), p. 5].

On the other side, Lincoln, in nearly every one of his
principal speeches, appealed to the authentic Revolutionary tradition. His most succinct statement was, of course,
in the familiar opening of the Gettysburg Address, to
which I have already referred in another connection.
But he rang all the rhetorical changes on this appeal, as,
for example, in his speech at Peoria in 1854:

> Our republican robe is soiled and trailed in the dust. Let us
> repurify it. Let us turn and wash it white in the spirit, if not
> the blood, of the Revolution. Let us turn slavery from its claims
> of "moral right" back upon its existing legal rights and its argu-
> ment of "necessity." Let us return it to the position our fathers
> gave it, and there let it rest in peace. Let us readopt the Declara-
> tion of Independence, and with it the practices and policy which
> harmonize with it.

Statesmen of the North were perhaps more inclined to
appeal to the Declaration of Independence, while those
of the South leaned more heavily on the Constitution.
But both had in common the assumption that the pretty
homogeneous philosophy of the Founding Fathers was
what they were being called upon to vindicate. Fitzhugh
did, to be sure, characterize the Declaration as "exhuber-
antly false, and arborescently fallacious." Yet even the
Declaration of Independence was by no means generally
rejected by southern advocates. Some southerners, for
example, Chief Justice Taney in the Dred Scott decision,
even argued that their position had been well stated in

the Declaration. They adduced historical proof (in my opinion convincing) that the authors of the sacred document had intended that Negroes be excluded from their professions of "equality." Another remarkable feature of the Dred Scott decision for us is the frankness with which it takes a preformation or a static view of the Constitution. Chief Justice Taney seemed to assume that the legal question of Negro status could be resolved by accurate historical definition of the original meaning of the Declaration of Independence and the Constitution, considered together.

Few documents could be more interesting in this connection than one which nowadays is almost never read. For there is probably no more authentic index to the theoretical conservatism of the "rebel" cause than the Constitution of the Confederate States of America. President Jefferson Davis boasted that the document proved the "conservative" temper of the people of the Confederate States. Alexander Stephens, his vice-president, declared that the form of the document showed that "their only leading object was to sustain, uphold, and perpetuate the fundamental principles of the Constitution of the United States." Closely following the original in organization, the Confederate constitution is almost a verbatim copy of the federal Constitution.

Its differences consist mainly in that it incorporates into the body of the document some of the principal amendments to the federal Constitution (the Bill of Rights, for example, being absorbed into Art. I, sec. 9); and it explicitly resolves certain ambiguities (for example, those concerning slavery and the federal principle generally) in the sense which the South believed to have been the original intent of the authors. The Preamble, for example, reads:

We, the People of the Confederate States, each State acting in its sovereign and independent character, in order to form a permanent Federal Government, establish justice, insure domestic tranquility, and secure the blessings of liberty to ourselves and our posterity—invoking the favor and guidance of Almighty God—do ordain and establish this Constitution for the Confederate States of America.

It is of great significance that in our bloody Civil War the so-called "rebel" side produced, through two of its best minds, treatises on the origin and nature of our Constitution which deserve to stand, alongside *The Federalist* and Adams' *Defence of the Constitutions,* on the small shelf of basic books about the American political system. The first, of course, is Calhoun's "Discourse on the Constitution and Government of the United States" (1851), which I have already described. The second is Alexander H. Stephens' *Constitutional View of the Late War between the States* (1868–70).

We cannot be surprised that the South, weaker in economy and in arms, found an incentive to be stronger in legal debate. But it remains a curiosity of political thought, as well as a pregnant fact of American history, that the principal theoretical defense of the southern position should have been a treatise on the origin of the federal Constitution, produced actually *after* the South had lost the last battle. Stephens' work was dedicated to "All true friends of the Union under the Constitution of the United

States, throughout their entire limits, without regard to present or past party associations." The conflict, Stephens emphasized, was not basically over slavery but over two "different and opposing ideas as to the nature of what is known as the General Government. The contest was between those who held it to be strictly Federal in its character, and those who maintained that it was thoroughly National." The work is historical: a documented demonstration that the Constitution was intended to set up a *federal* government.

We can begin to grasp the true proportions of what I have called the continuity of the history of the United States, as contrasted with that of the countries of western Europe, if we try to imagine the leader of a defeated party in any of the recent European civil wars producing a heavy scholarly treatise proving that he had been in the right *strictly from the point of view of constitutional theory*. George Fitzhugh in 1857 and Jefferson Davis in 1881 both earnestly wished for the "strength and perpetuity" of the Union.

In virtually every one of the recent domestic struggles in Europe, the conflict has been so basic that only one side could conceivably have set itself up as the champion of existing legal institutions. The other has proudly stood for a new concept of government, for a new constitution, and another basis of law. Hitler's cynicism toward the German constitution is typical of this frame of mind. Yet in the American Civil War, after hundreds of thousands of lives had been lost, both sides were still thinking on similar constitutional assumptions. An intelligent and realistic critic like Alexander Stephens still after the war considered it possible that his image of the original doctrine (that the Union was a federal and not a national government) might eventually prevail. This hope would have been hardly conceivable, had not both parties to the conflict accepted the same premises of political theory, had they not preserved a common devotion to a hypothetically perfect original theory. This is what I mean by the idea of "preformation."

For the reasons which I have mentioned, the legacy of the Civil War to American thought has been one of sectionalism and constitutional debate rather than of dogmatic nationalism and "return to fundamentals." The tendency of sectionalism has been to reinforce our awareness of variety within our national culture and of the desirability and inevitability of preserving it. The tendency of the continuous constitutional tradition has been to give the defeated cause, the South, a legitimate theoretical position within the federal system.

The South, except in its romantic literature of chivalry and mint juleps, is now no champion of a different concept of life but rather of a different constitutional emphasis. The South remains, as it is desirable that someone should always be, champion of the states'-rights, local-autonomy principle of our federal Constitution. The South can still debate about what it once gave its lives to defend, for it has never lost essential devotion to the constitutional spirit and its pure original image. What Lincoln called "the spirit of concession and compromise, that spirit which has never failed us in past perils, and which may be safely trusted for all the future"—that spirit can survive precisely because the Civil War was poor in political theory. Notwithstanding the abolitionists and people like Garrison who wished to burn the Constitution, the war did not represent a quest for a general redefinition of political values.

Whatever the crimes, the senseless bitterness, that were visited on the South in the era of reconstruction, they were committed in a vindictive or narrowly provincial spirit. The triumph of the national emphasis in the federal structure did not carry with it victory of a nationalist philosophy. In Lincoln's phrase, "the Union"—not any self-conscious national culture—was what was to be preserved. This distinguished him sharply from his contemporaries like Bismarck and Cavour. The remarkable reintegration of the South into our constitutional system is the best evidence of the community of certain assumptions. The Civil War emerged, then, as a struggle over complicated matters, on which everyone knew there had been a long series of compromises, beginning with the Declaration of Independence and the Constitution themselves. Such a controversy could have happened only within the framework of going federal institutions.

Not the least remarkable feature of the Civil War apart from the fact that it occurred at all—is that it was so unproductive of political theory. This, the bloodiest single civil war of the nineteenth century, was also perhaps the least theoretical. The sectional character of the conflict had tended to make sociology—the description of things as they were—take the place of the uncharted exploration of things as they ought to be. It also prevented the crisis from propagating panaceas. This was another example of the recurrent tendency in American history to identify the "is" with the "ought," to think of values and a theory of society as implicit in facts about society. The era was strikingly lacking in romanticism of the Rousseauistic brand. The romantics of the day were the Thaddeus Stevenses—the bearers of fire and sword.

At the same time, the federal character of the struggle, the fact that it took place within a functioning federal order, confined much of the theoretical discussion within the area of constitutional law, of the search for the true original image of the Constitution. This, too, discouraged American thinkers of the age (excepting a vagrant Thoreau) from making confusion in the market place an excuse for going off into the solitude of the woods to rethink the whole problem of institutions. The sense of "givenness" was reinforced. In this case it meant the empirical tradition, the reliance on constitutionalism, and an unwillingness to remake institutions out of whole cloth.

The continuity of American political thought—which included the American way of *not* philosophizing about politics—was to stay. The mere fact that the nation had survived the ordeal of civil war seemed itself to prove the strength of the thread which bound the present to the past and to confirm the common destiny of the nation.

V

THE MINGLING OF POLITICAL AND
RELIGIOUS THOUGHT

IN THE preceding chapters I showed how three crises
in our national history illustrate certain characteristics
of our political thought. Through the Puritans, the American Revolution, and the Civil War, I have tried to un-
derline the ways in which peculiarities of our history
have encouraged our belief in "givenness." Many facts
about our past have nourished this belief that an elaborate
or outspoken political theory was superfluous for us, on
the simple ground that we already possessed a theory.
Explicit political philosophy has seemed unnecessary precisely because our history and our institutions have
seemed to contain an implicit political philosophy adequate to all our needs. We have drawn values out of
"facts." We have been empirical and legalistic rather than
metaphysical and ethical in debating our national crises.
All this has led us to homogenize our past, to push John
Winthrop and Thomas Jefferson into the single category
of Founding Fathers, to think of "the North" against "the
South."

In the present chapter I will abandon the chronological
treatment. Instead of examining a particular crisis, I will
describe two general characteristics of our culture, both

of which express that belief in "givenness" which I described in the first chapter. First, our tendency to break down the boundaries between different systems of belief: as, for example, between religious sects or between religious and political thought. Second, our tendency to be voluble: to wear our heart on our sleeve, to try to say what we believe. Perhaps it is because we have been unclear in our theoretical distinctions that we have talked a lot about our beliefs.

By the mingling of religious and political thought I mean, then, only another example of our willingness to gloss over philosophic distinctions: the distinctions both among religious sects and between all religious thought and all political thought. Belief in "givenness" has made this possible. Because we believe that we do share certain automatically defined values, our inability to sharpen our philosophy has seemed no evidence of a lack of common faith. Finally, it will appear that this glossing-over of distinctions has itself provided us additional incentives to cling to our belief in "givenness."

I. AMERICAN RELIGION AND THE TWO-PARTY SYSTEM

Religion is traditionally a realm where values become symbolized and speak out. Moreover, as we know it in modern western European culture, religion is sectarian. It is at least one area of life in which Americans would seem, then, to find themselves willy-nilly tied to a comprehensive, outspoken, and differentiated philosophy. What have we done with this doctrinal inheritance?

The present situation in the United States is pretty well

described in the words which Gibbon used in his *Decline and Fall of the Roman Empire* to characterize religion in that other happily tolerant era, the age of the Antonines. "The various modes of worship which prevailed in the Roman world," Gibbon observed (chap. ii), "were all considered by the people as equally true; by the philosopher as equally false; and by the magistrate as equally useful. And thus toleration produced not only mutual indulgence, but even religious concord." The United States in our generation is the rival of the Roman Empire in the number of its religious sects, in the candor of its religious toleration, and in the depth and generality of the belief that religion is the bulwark of society. If we cannot rival the diversity of Roman religions, from Isis and Mithra at one extreme to Christianity and Judaism at the other, we can perhaps excel her in the number of our sects, in the minuteness of the differences between them, and in the elaborateness of their organization.

But while religion flourishes in this country, theology and religious studies languish. The various religious bodies in the United States claim a membership of almost ninety million; they receive no little support in wealth and energy. You cannot find a town so small that it is without a church or a city where religious buildings are not prominent. The chapel is invariably among the most conspicuous—and most expensive—buildings on any American university campus. The University of Chicago, for example, possesses a chapel which is said to have cost $2,280,000 in 1928; calculated per square footage of floor space, this is probably the most costly building on the campus, not excepting the institutes of atomic research. Throughout the country there is a vast disproportion between the wealth and energy devoted to religious buildings and religious activity, on the one hand, and the time and energy devoted to theology or to anything that could even loosely be called religious thought.

Intellectually speaking, "religions" are unimportant in American life; but Religion is of enormous importance. To conform in the United States, it is important to be a member of *a* church (and in "church" the American would, of course, include the Catholic church and the Jewish synagogue). Which particular church is far less important (provided, of course, it is *not* a Catholic church or a Jewish synagogue). We all knew that President Truman went to church; most of us would not want a president who did not. But few of us actually know to what denomination he belongs.

Our leading national heroes, Washington and Lincoln, have both been noted in American tradition for their religiosity. Yet neither was a prominent member of any particular denomination. In the case of Washington it is not easy to prove that he was a Christian in the theological sense. Nevertheless, their religious spirit has become a traditional part of their historic image. We thus assume that a man—even a leader—can be religious, and actually Christian, without any clear theology. Our coins bear the inscription "In God We Trust," which is as precise theologically as the religions of our great men.

Ex-Governor Adlai Stevenson recently made a confession which comes close to laying bare the heart of our problem. "If it's true that politics is the art of compromise," he said, "I've had a good start; my mother was a Republican and a Unitarian, my father was a Democrat and a Presbyterian. I ended up in his party and her church" (*Time*, January 28, 1952). The implication is, of course, that in the United States there is no more difference between the creeds of the Unitarian and the Presbyterian churches than between the platforms of the Democratic and the Republican parties. Such a view would hardly salve the spirits of Michael Servetus, John Knox, and William Ellery Channing. But actually, as politicians often do, Mr. Stevenson said a great deal more than he intended, because the fact which makes possible such an attitude toward religious denominations is the same one that accounts for our two-party system. This is nothing other than the remarkable agreement on social values in the United States, rooted in our sense of "givenness."

What I mean will become obvious by comparison with the domestic politics of the countries of western Europe. The small ideological difference between our two political parties may be accounted for by the fact that their only disagreement is over means. Both Democrats and Republicans have, on the whole, the same vision of the kind of society there ought to be in the United States. They differ only over whether that kind of society is more likely to be attained by much or little aid to western Europe, by much or little regulation of labor unions, by one or another form of taxation—or by Republicans or Democrats holding office.

But in many other ostensibly democratic countries—for example, Italy or France—the disagreement among major parties is of a very different character. There, as has often been observed, politics is the realm of ends, in which the citizen asserts whether his society should realize Catholic principles or Communist principles or any one of a dozen other concepts of social justice. In Europe men are more intransigent about politics because their politics is concerned with a more basic question: What shall be the ends of society?

In a country like Italy, for example, the political debate expresses nothing less than disagreement about the nature of "the good life" and "the good society." To talk to the people there is an education in the variety of concepts which sane people can hold of the proper ends of society. Their theories are as various as the colors of the rainbow—sometimes, also, as indistinct. By talking politics with enough of these people, one acquires an index to ideology and political values: anarchism, chauvinism, communism, fascism, monarchism, socialism, syndicalism, and a host of others—even to xenophobia. In such a situation the religious element in political life is divisive. It does not express ends which all accept and seek to realize through politics. Rather it is simply another way of expressing disagreement over ends. And in a disintegrating society politics becomes a controversy over ends.

None of this is true in the United States. Here the number of people who do not accept the predominant values of our society is negligible. Politics here has therefore seldom, if ever, been the realm of ends. The good life on the new continent was to be no product of any articulate vision of society but rather, as we have seen, of the conditions—or perhaps the magic—of the New World itself. However crudely or unsuccessfully articulated, the ends of society in America have nevertheless been generally agreed upon. The disagreement among American political parties, with only a few exceptions, has been over the practical question of how to secure the agreed objective, while conciliating different interests, rather than over ultimate values or over what interest is paramount. Therefore, American political life has been characterized both by less theoretical clarity and by less intransigence and acrimony than one would find in France, Italy, or Germany.

The same has been true of our religious life. Because no particular religious sect has ever been in a position to dominate our national life, our starting point, in this, as in many other areas, has been diversity. The Reformation and the religious wars are, happily, events of European and not of American history. England, France, and Germany each possesses a strong and articulate spirit of religious dissent, arising partly from the fact that the point of departure in their early modern history was religious uniformity (or at least "cuius regio, eius religio"). But we actually started from the necessity of not allowing sectarian diversity to interfere with national unity. And this partly because of the fact that for a long time we had established religions in our separate states.

The two-party system and what I shall call "non-denominationalism" in religion both express our fundamental agreement. The same reason why we have produced very little speculative political theory is why we have not been concerned with basic doctrinal issues in religion. There is already so much agreement. It is not intellectually enticing to explore what is already known or supposed to be known, or what is so generally agreed upon as to seem commonplace or obvious.

II. CHARACTERISTICS OF AMERICAN RELIGION

The specific characteristics of this peculiarly American approach to religion, which I shall now consider, were suggested by De Tocqueville in his *Democracy in America* (Vol. II, Book I, chap. i) a century ago:

It must never be forgotten that religion gave birth to Anglo-American society. In the United States, religion is therefore mingled with all the habits of the nation and all the feelings of patriotism, whence it derives a peculiar force. . . . Christianity has . . . retained a strong hold on the public mind in America . . . its sway is not only that of a philosophical doctrine which has been adopted upon inquiry, but of a religion which is believed without discussion. In the United States, Christian sects are infinitely diversified and perpetually modified; but Christianity itself is an established and irresistible fact, which no one undertakes either to attack or to defend [trans. Henry Reeve (New York, 1946), II, 6].

Some of the reasons why the diversity of dogmas has not been emphasized and why an unexamined generalized religion has become so firmly established may appear from the characteristics which most of our religions have in common.

For our purpose, it will suffice to recall those features which happen to show how religion in the United States has been subordinated to and blended with the generally accepted values of the community. During this oversimplified summary, one should bear in mind that special qualifications might be required in relation to those religions like Catholicism and orthodox Judaism, which, for one reason or another, have been less assimilated, less Americanized. More of that later. With this qualification, we might enumerate the following pretty obvious characteristics of religions in the United States. Each of them is another way of glossing over theoretical distinctions.

1. Religions are *instrumental*. They commend themselves to us for the services they perform more than for the truths which they affirm. This is, of course, exemplified in the fact that, on the whole in this country (with the exceptions of Jews and Catholics), greater importance is attached to the local congregation of which one is a member than to the larger church, denomination, or confession. When a Protestant American family moves from one neighborhood or one city to another, it often selects its new church affiliation on the basis of which congregation can offer the social activities and personal services which it expects. Even Judaism—or at least its reformed branch—has become pretty well assimilated to this instrumental emphasis. One Jewish congregation has for the motto of its Sunday School, "Sinai never does things halfway." Where could one find a more literal translation of what William James calls "the instinctive belief of mankind: God is real since he produces real effects." When the reformed rabbi writes to his congregation urging the observance of the Sabbath, he points out

the many advantages of such observance, not only for adding beauty to the home environment, but, he implies, for holding the family together ("Families that pray together, stay together"), for keeping the children out of mischief, for lowering one's blood pressure, and for securing release from nervous tension.

A familiar illustration of this instrumentalist emphasis in Protestantism is the so-called "Community Church" movement. Aiming to provide a "religious" center for the local residents of all denominations, it is headquarters for the Boy Scouts, for lecture series, for basketball games, and for opportunities to meet other nice people.

The most sophisticated, and also perhaps the most honest, expression of this instrumental approach to religion is found in John Dewey's quest for what he calls "the religious in experience." As he writes in his little book, significantly entitled *A Common Faith*, he wishes that "whatever is basically religious in experience had the opportunity to express itself free from all historic encumbrances." By "historic encumbrances" he means specific theological beliefs. "I believe," Dewey says, "that many persons are so repelled from what exists as a religion by its intellectual and moral implications, that they are not even aware of attitudes in themselves that if they came to fruition would be genuinely religious." And he therefore concludes: "The actual religious quality in the experience described is the *effect* produced, the better adjustment in life and its conditions, not the manner and cause of its production. The way in which the experience operated, its function, determines its religious value."

2. Religions are *personal*. This attitude is, in one sense, simply an aspect of the instrumental view, for it emphasizes the service which religion can perform for the individual. But it is something more, too, for it implies a notion of the *kind* of service which religions ought to perform, and it involves a special view of the relation between man and God. It is the assumption that, properly and normally, religion is to be subordinated to the need of the individual personality.

A study of religion, then, might very well be (in William James's phrase) a study of "Man's Religious Appetites," these appetites presumably being as much individualized as any others. In the background looms the "De gustibus . . ." which is one way of expressing indifference, toleration, and respectability. Our center of interest is certainly not religious doctrine, "not religious institutions, but rather religious feelings and religious impulses."

We have an admirable statement of this kind of interest in William James's important book, *Varieties of Religious Experience*. From this point of view the truth of religions becomes irrelevant. "Religion . . . ," James concludes, "cannot be a mere anachronism and survival, but must exert a permanent function, whether she be with or without intellectual content, and whether, if she have any, it be true or false." But what of the content of religions? "Is there," he asks, "under all the discrepancies of the creeds, a common nucleus to which they bear their testimony unanimously?"

James immediately answers, Yes. The common nucleus proves to be something intensely personal, and if per-

forming a uniform function, still a function in each case
uniquely adapted to the need of each individual:

> The warring gods and formulas of the various religions do
> indeed cancel each other, but there is a certain uniform deliver-
> ance in which religions all appear to meet. It consists of two
> parts: 1. An uneasiness; and 2. Its solution.
> 1. The uneasiness, reduced to its simplest terms, is a sense that
> there is *something wrong about us* as we naturally stand.
> 2. The solution is a sense that *we are saved from the wrong-
> ness* by making proper connection with the higher powers [*Vari-
> eties of Religious Experience* ("Modern Library"), p. 498].

How each of us resolves his personal uneasiness is, then,
his particular brand of religion.

This personal quality of religion is manifested not
merely in such a familiar recent phenomenon as the identification of religion with "peace of mind" and release
from nervous tension, but also in a quaint paradox in our
religious life. Although, at least for the last century, theology and religious dogma have been unimportant in our
national life, somehow or other sectarianism has seemed
to flourish.

When Mrs. Trollope visited this country in 1828, she
was already amazed by our sectarianism. As she wrote in
her *Domestic Manners of the Americans* (chap. xi),
what she saw here proved that "a religious tyranny may
be exerted very effectually without the aid of the government, and in a way much more oppressive than the
paying of tithe, and without obtaining any of the salu-
tary decorum . . . of an established mode of worship."
She was shocked to see Americans "insisting upon having

each a little separate banner, embroidered with a device of their own imagining":

> The whole people appear to be divided into an almost endless variety of religious factions. . . . Besides the broad and well-known distinctions of Episcopalian, Roman Catholic, Presbyterian, Calvinist, Baptist, Quaker, Swedenborgian, Universalist, Dunker, &c., &c., &c., there are innumerable others springing out of these, each of which assumes a church government of its own; of this, the most intriguing and factious individual is invariably the head; and in order, as it should seem, to show a reason for this separation, each congregation invests itself with some queer variety of external observance that has the melancholy effect of exposing *all* religious ceremonies to contempt [(New York, 1904), pp. 95 f.].

Where sects are so numerous, the differences between them, paradoxically, become less important. They need not quarrel or even debate with one another—although they can indeed compete in the size and wealth of their congregations. It is enough if each serves the personal need of its member and helps him quiet his particular kind of uneasiness.

The fact that, as I have mentioned, the religion of Washington or Lincoln was nondescript, or purely personal, would thus seem no denial of the truly religious spirit of each of them. We assume, on the contrary, that the greater the man, the stronger his individuality, the more likely that he would need a religion tailor-made to his personality.

3. *Non-denominationalism.* The upshot has been a phenomenon in the United States which might be called "non-denominationalism" or belief in a generalized re-

145

ligion. This belief was admirably expressed in a recent statement by President Eisenhower. "I am the most intensely religious man I know," the President observed. "That doesn't mean I adhere to any sect. A democracy cannot exist without a religious base. I believe in democracy" (*Chicago Daily News*, January 12, 1952).

Since the interfaith ceremonies of emperor-worship under the Roman Empire, there has probably never been a comparable submersion of separate religious beliefs in a common generalized religion. Our so-called "interfaith" religious activities (exemplified by the National Conference of Christians and Jews, etc.) are supposed to show the vitality of religion in general; they are also often ceremonies of a vaguely patriotic character. Our national holidays have this non-denominational, yet distinctly religious, character. Thanksgiving Day, which has no significance if not religious, is the best example. But there is a host of others, including Easter, Christmas, Memorial Day, and Armistice Day, and certainly such events as Brotherhood Week and Mother's Day. A non-denominational ritualism accompanies the sessions of Congress and state legislatures and the inaugurations of presidents and governors.

Such facts sometimes shock foreign visitors, especially from France. There, freedom of religion is taken to include the freedom to be an atheist and the separation of church and state implies the separation of the state from *all* religion, not merely from any particular religion. French observers are even more shocked when they learn that in many public schools in the United States there is daily reading of the Bible and sometimes prayers. American parents consider these acceptable or even desirable and seldom object, provided that the reading is from the Old Testament.

Notwithstanding Cotton Mather, the Know-Nothings, the Ku Klux Klan, Paul Blanshard, and The Brooklyn Tablet, we have been distinguished from western Europe by our avoidance of religious strife. This is partly a result of our distinctive ability to produce a kind of elixir, sometimes vapid and always unpungent, a blended distillate of all our different religions. In his *American Language*, H. L. Mencken tells us that, as we might have expected, the vague phrase "to get (or experience) religion" is an American invention. The conception of a generalized religion is perhaps a peculiarity of our culture: the combined product of our genuine religiosity, the diversity of our religious institutions, and our basic agreement on community values.

This generalized religion is itself virtually without dogma. It is as far as possible from anything like pantheism, or even from anything as undogmatic as humanism. What it is, is the lowest common denominator of all presently accepted and respectable institutional religions found within the borders of our country.

One of the significant consequences of this tendency to generalize religion is its effect in the United States on the character of those few religions—like Roman Catholicism, Judaism, and the uncompromising minor Protestant sects—which have remained socially or doctrinally unassimilated. In the United States such groups are distinguished from others not merely by the content of their dogma, but more significantly by the fact that they insist (in a way sometimes considered bad taste) on any doctrine at all. In contrast with the hazy outlines of the generalized religion, the sharp profile of any particular doctrine appears sharper still. Therefore, for example, the individual American Catholic is perhaps even more aware of his commitment than is the case in Italy, where everybody is Catholic, or in France, where all religions have clearer dogmatic outlines.

In American culture, then, an especially valuable role may be reserved for those religions like Judaism, Catholicism, and the intransigent Protestant sects which remain in a sense "un-American" because they have not yet completely taken on the color of their environment. Such sects, while accepting the moral premises of the community, can still try to judge the community by some standard outside its own history. But even these religions often take on a peculiar American complexion and tend toward validating themselves by their accord with things as they are.

In this connection, we have a revealing document in Alfred E. Smith's reply in April, 1927, to the accusation that his membership in the Roman Catholic church was incompatible with his loyalty to the United States government. In the most effective, most engaging, and most American passage of his reply he remarks:

Everything that has actually happened to me during my long public career leads me to know that no such thing as that [the incompatibility between Catholicism and Americanism] is true. I have taken an oath of office in this State nineteen times. Each time I swore to defend and maintain the Constitution of the United States. All of this represents a period of public service in elective office almost continuous since 1903. I have never known any conflict between my official duties and my religious belief. No such conflict could exist. Certainly the people of this State recognize no such conflict. They have testified to my devotion to public duty by electing me to the highest office within their gift four times [*Atlantic Monthly*, CXXXIX (1927), 722].

Such a forthright and empirical defense to a doctrinal charge would seem irrelevant in the political controversy of almost any European country.

III. THAT WE TALK MUCH AND SAY LITTLE
ABOUT OUR BELIEFS

Our tendency to break down the boundaries between different systems of belief, which I have described, has been encouraged by the notion that there is some larger, unspoken, and perhaps unutterable common belief which underlies them all. A second general expression of our belief in "givenness," to which I shall now turn, is our talkativeness. It is our tendency to talk about, or perhaps more precisely to "brag" about, what we believe, without troubling with technicalities like definitions.

Its purest, if most extreme, expression is what has come to be called "the spread-eagle style," characterized by one writer as "a compound of exaggeration, effrontery, bombast, and extravagance, mixed metaphors, platitudes, defiant threats thrown at the world, and irreverent appeals flung at the Supreme Being." Anyone who knows the *Congressional Record* could not accuse us of coyness about our national faith. The American is notoriously voluble and unreserved in his speech, not only about personal matters, but about what he takes to be his philosophy.

What is the connection between the inarticulateness of our political thought, which I have described in earlier chapters, and this volubleness of our political talkers and writers? Perhaps never before in history has a people talked so much and said so little about its basic beliefs. Perhaps never before has a people been fuller of pledges and creeds and oaths, of high-sounding speeches and worthy maxims and mottoes. Nor have these ever before been so widely diffused—on the mastheads of newspapers, on the walls of grocery stores and filling stations and insurance offices; over the apple pie of the Rotary Club and the aspic of the Country Club; out of the image of Charlie Chaplin (or "Monsieur Verdoux") or Claude Rains or Edward G. Robinson on the motion-picture screen; or out of the mouth of W. J. Cameron or Walter Winchell over the radio; from countless, endless voices in the halls of Congress; and now from countless faces on television.

It would be futile for us to deny that a tendency to talk about what we believe is a national characteristic. The reaction of some cynical spirits is exemplified in the comment of Sam Goldwyn of Hollywood on the script of a movie which ended with a familiar exhortation to high ideals: "If you wanna send a message, use Western Union." A fair comparison with other peoples or other times will show that most of us are inordinately fond of hearing ourselves or others talk about what we believe.

These statements, as I mentioned in the opening chapter, are hopelessly inadequate formulations of what we really believe, of what is characteristic in our institutions. Yet their quantity shows our need for *some* articulation of our beliefs and our awareness of the groping inadequacy in each of the endless attempts. The American Heritage Foundation, in its recent *Program To Promote National Unity and Morale* proposed:

> On July 4, 1951 delegates from each of the forty-eight states (delegates appointed by the Governor) will gather in Independence Hall, Philadelphia, and after studying the various community Re-Declarations, will draft and approve a national Re-Declaration of Faith in the American Dream.
>
> Proclaiming this significant event, the original Liberty Bell in Philadelphia, and Liberty Bells throughout the land will ring—as a dramatic symbol of national unity and high morale, and as a gesture of defiance to the Enemy.

While we have filled libraries with grandiloquent and hollow verbiage about our ideals, we have produced precious few profound and enduring books of political philosophy. At the same time—and this fact should never be out of sight—we have offered the world an unprecedented example of successful federal representative institutions.

The vagueness and inarticulateness which I have already pointed out in our religions has not kept them from being voluble. No one could complain that sermons are too short, that ministers do not express themselves frequently enough, that their invocations on public occasions are not sufficiently long, that there are not enough radio programs of a vaguely religious character, or enough books of a "healing" and religiously inspiring complexion. We have had, if one wants to call them that, our "Acres of Diamonds," and more than our share of Elbert Hubbards and Bruce Bartons. The spectacular success of the Chautauqua experiment was largely in this area of the "healing" volubleness—appealing to what William James charitably called "earnest and helpless minds." Popular religious novels like *Ben Hur, Quo Vadis, The Robe, The Silver Chalice*, and paraphrases of the Bible like *The Greatest Story Ever Told* have become best sellers.

In short, it would be hard to say that Americans have not been offered much to satisfy what James called the "religious appetite." Nor could one deny that the food and drink have been notoriously diluted. Recently, we have been about as barren of articulate religious thought, with the conspicuous exception of a few stimulating scholars like Irving Babbitt and Reinhold Niebuhr, as we have been prodigal of words about religion.

Nor, strangely enough, has the sheer number and ostensible diversity of our religious denominations helped sharpen our beliefs. In this country, as contrasted with England, for example, the several denominations have not been whetstones for one another. Here, rather, we have engaged in a search for a kind of lowest common denominator.

Perhaps the existence of an amorphous lowest common denominator has itself removed much of the incentive (and some of the need) to find precise theoretical formulation. Our feeling of agreement, together with the absence of a special class of articulators of the agreement (such as one finds in an aristocratic or priestly society) and the lack of satisfactory philosophical explorations of the bases of our society, has stimulated our need to assert and to hear asserted the simple *fact* of our agreement. Or is this nothing but an effort to make up in quantity of words what is lacking in subtlety of thought? I refuse to believe what was suggested to me by an English friend recently, that all this is due to the "immaturity" of our culture.

It would be easy to multiply examples of the characteristic American attempt to be explicit and articulate about the national values. We try to say in a public speech, or in a framed motto on an office wall, what other cultures think fit subjects for priests or political philosophers. We are all familiar with our emphasis on creeds and oaths of loyalty. The recent controversies over loyalty oaths are perhaps less significant for the content of the oaths than for the widely accepted assumption that the essence of patriotic belief can be contained in an oath or a ceremonial affirmation.

When as a boy I attended public high school in Oklahoma, our school assemblies were regularly preceded by formulas in the following order: pledge of allegiance to the flag of the United States, singing of the "Star Spangled Banner," singing of the state anthem, recitation of the "Student's Creed" (which went: "I believe in honest work, generous comradeship and the courage of high convictions . . ."), recitation of the "Student's Prayer," and reading of a passage from the Bible. This was often climaxed by an inspirational talk.

Commencement ceremonies, which now mark the completion of all phases of education from the university down to the nursery school, are occasions for iteration of our group ideals. Service clubs, like Rotary, Optimist, Lions, Kiwanis, and many others, make the recitation of a credo followed by an inspirational address a common feature of their meetings. The enormous success of magazines like the *Reader's Digest* (9,000,000 circulation, the largest in the country) rests on their skill in ringing the changes on American ideals.

Or consider our holidays. The multiplication of holidays in the United States should not be dismissed as the mere commercialization of sentiment. It is equally evidence of a self-conscious quest for simple and outspoken statements of values. And here we reach a high level of explicitness found nowhere else. Such an occasion as Mother's Day or Father's Day (incredible to the European observer) is perhaps the most extreme example of our willingness to talk about our intimate beliefs. Expressing affection for one's mother is assumed to be no more complex or private than pinning a carnation on one's lapel.

Our American college president, who is supposed to be a kind of academic edition of the *Reader's Digest*, is unique in the world of education. Generally speaking, he is neither a citizen of eminence, like the Chancellor of an English university, nor a member of the faculty serving a tour of administrative duty, as in many Continental universities. Apart from his roles as presidential-candidate and fund-raiser, he is a kind of professional talker about community ideals. His field of specialization is "uplift," which, by the way, is a word of American invention.

In this connection we should not overlook the exuberant development of oratory in the United States. The obvious explanation, like Thoreau's, that "we love eloquence for its own sake, and not for any truth which it may utter, or any heroism it may inspire," seems to me inadequate. Despite the flourishing of American oratory, we have, at least for a century or so, shown very little interest in the separate study of rhetoric (unless we choose to put books like Dale Carnegie's in that class). The peculiar importance of oratory in American life—and that importance has, of course, taken on new dimensions with radio and television—is not explained by a sheer love of the operatic and flamboyant. Few would call this a quality of the American national character. Rather it expresses our national desire for affirmation. The fact that the foundations of our belief have not been articulated in the works of philosophers makes us all the more anxious for some everyday expression of our sense of community.

Perhaps in no other modern country has oratory been more profusely developed. We can list a Webster, a Calhoun, a Lincoln, and a Franklin D. Roosevelt. But public speaking in the United States is probably less significant as an art than as an institution. We have had a considerable number of men like Henry Clay, Robert G. Ingersoll, Clarence Darrow, Huey Long, and Father Coughlin, who (in the phrase of one historian of American oratory) actually "talked themselves into national prominence."

In the popular mind and in school textbooks, American history is recounted at least as much in the series of notable public utterances which have sought to give explicit expression to American political ideals as in any other kind of event. Collections of great American orations have been a widespread popular substitute for narrative history.

It would not be difficult to compile a complete American history which would give the substance of what is now taught in our public school courses in history through the most dramatic and effective public speeches. Such a volume would include: James Otis' speech against the writs of assistance, Patrick Henry's "Give Me Liberty or Give Me Death," Washington's First Inaugural Address, Jefferson's First Inaugural Address, a selection of speeches by Clay and Calhoun, the Webster-Hayne debate, the Lincoln-Douglas debates, a few speeches by Wendell Phillips, Lincoln's First and Second Inaugural Addresses and the Gettysburg Address, Bryan's "Cross of Gold," some speeches of Theodore Roosevelt, Wilson's First Inaugural Address, Franklin D. Roosevelt's First Inaugural Address and some of his radio speeches. We can find few nations whose oratory can bring the student so close to their history. The famous Fourth of July oration is not simply an example of the dilution of

American literature; it is actually an important institution, a touchstone of American political thought.

IV. THE SEARCH FOR THE COMMON DENOMINATOR: THE MINGLING OF POLITICS AND RELIGION

The characteristics of our thought which I have been describing in the present chapter show a quaint inversion of the Quaker way of agreement. Quakers seek to arrive at the sense of the meeting through silence, through each individual's affirming what his spirit moves him to affirm. A group of Americans seeks to arrive at agreement through talk, through each individual's trying to put into words what the community already believes.

Whether all this talk is capable of *producing* agreement is really not too important, if, as I have suggested, the agreement is there all the time. Much of what passes for public debate in the United States is, then, less an attempt to tell people what to think than to state what everybody already thinks. One of the reasons why we are willing—or even eager—to commit our social philosophy to a search for the lowest common denominator is simply that we are so sure that the agreement is already there, that the common denominator really exists.

The tendency to gloss over differences and construct a kind of generalized American religion, and the tendency to talk a great deal about what we believe without feeling the obligation to sharpen our definitions—both of these express a unity in American life. They also show our tendency to break down another distinction familiar in European countries: between the public and the private areas of life.

When we have broken down the boundaries between public and private life, between community values and personal belief, between political philosophy and religious faith, we have prepared ourselves to make the agreed-upon community values do for a religious doctrine. The "givenness" of community values then seems to relieve us of the need to formulate personal values. Under these circumstances, it is not surprising that we are anxious to state even our private ideals in a form to which all could assent—to develop a kind of generalized American religion. We have, then, carried our spirit of compromise over from action into thought. Starting from the view that different creeds can live peaceably together, we gradually come to the notion that, if creeds can live together, they must be fundamentally similar.

In a curious and altogether characteristic way the currents of our religious and our political feelings mix. In more theologically minded countries, sharp theological doctrines actually help define the boundaries of *religious* sentiment; similarly, in such countries the definitions of political theory help separate a special field of *political* doctrine. But in the United States religious and political thought overflow into each other. We have already observed some of the consequences of this intermingling both for religion and for politics.

Here each of the two areas of thought, the political and the religious, seeks to compensate for the vagueness and inadequacy of the other by being still more explicit, without necessarily becoming more precise. Thus we expect, on the one hand, that a political speech should have "uplift" or some personally inspiring drift to it and, on the other hand, that a sermon should have some worthy social implication. For people who have no clear theology, there is no reason why political ideals should *not* be expected to supply the place of personal philosophy. For those who find it difficult to express their political ideals, there is no reason why they should not expect the deficiency to be made up by their religious preachers.

The more popular and influential preachers of our national ideals have stood midway between politics and religion: Franklin, Washington, Jefferson, Lincoln, Bryan, Theodore Roosevelt, Wilson, and even Franklin D. Roosevelt. Much of our political articulation is in this religio-political realm and could be taken equally as an example of what we have called a generalized religion or as an affirmation of political ideals: from the maxims of Poor Richard, Emerson's *Essays* ("Self-Reliance," for example), Whitman's *Leaves of Grass* and *Democratic Vistas*, to William Allen White's editorials and John Dos Passos' *U.S.A.* It is significant how large a proportion of our better literature occupies this middle ground between the area of personal religious quest and that of social definition and affirmation.

The private and the public have become one. What other country has considered its system of education a laboratory of democracy and has developed (as John Dewey did for us) a political theory in the form of a philosophy of education? What we say about ourselves, our ideals, and our society comes, then, from the whole texture of our life; we are as ill-qualified to speak of the political apart from the personal or religious aspect of life as we are to write treatises on theology or on political philosophy.

This makes it doubly difficult for us to communicate to other cultures, in any neat and intelligible fashion, the special qualities of our political institutions. Much of what passes for statement of our national ideals is, then, only a kind of talking to ourselves, a kind of ritual reassurance of our agreement. If we are whistling to keep up our courage, we must remember that the sounds we make may serve their purpose for us, and yet not seem music to anyone else.

VI

OUR CULTURAL HYPOCHONDRIA
AND HOW TO CURE IT

OUR indifference to grand theories has been possible partly because we have taken for granted that God himself drew the plans of our career and marked its outlines in our history and on our very ground. This is what I have called the sense of "givenness."

We have seen how, when a full-blown theory was actually brought here, as it was by the New England Puritans, the success of the community under American conditions tended to break that theory down. What one *could* build on this continent tended to become the criterion of what one ought to build here. We have also seen how the peculiar character of the American Revolution and of the Civil War made our soil unfertile for ranging speculation. The fact that the American Revolution was an affirmation of the ancient British constitution and that the Civil War was a conflict between constitutional orthodoxies has tended to fence in our political reflection, making lawyers take the place of political philosophers. Moreover, the sectional character of the Civil War, by encouraging comparisons of cultures as wholes, fed our tendency to make sociology do for political theory, to confound the "ought" and the "is."

In the preceding chapter we finally have seen how the circumstances of our life, interpreted by the axiom that we all actually have a common belief, have glossed over sectarian differences in religion and produced a kind of generalized, non-denominational faith. We have also seen how this kind of faith, taken together with the lack of distinctions in our political philosophy, has tended to break down the boundaries between religious and political thought. The American, therefore, has looked for a personal philosophy in his political values and has expected a political philosophy to be implied in his personal religion. I have pointed out how all this, along with our firm belief in "givenness," with the poverty of our political theory and the genuine community of our values, has led us to talk a great deal about our common faith without at the same time clarifying or defining it.

We thus find engraved in our national consciousness the belief that values have somehow emerged from the American experience; that we do not need American philosophers because we already have an American philosophy, implicit in the American Way of Life.

The belief in "givenness," which I have discussed in this book, is not unrelated to the more familiar idea of an American destiny, the notion that America has had a preordained role in the world. But the two ideas are by no means the same. What has in the past given a local flavor to our concept of destiny has been precisely that the destiny was to fulfil purposes which seemed impossible and/or unnecessary for any human mind to comprehend. "When one talks to an American of his national purpose," H. G. Wells remarked some years ago, "he seems a little at a loss; if one speaks of his national destiny, he responds with alacrity." The concept of destiny has been an ever deepening current in American thought. Conviction that America has a mission to mankind was perhaps never stronger than today.

I. THE DECLINING SENSE OF "GIVENNESS"

Some of the bewilderment in which we find ourselves is due to the fact that, while belief in destiny has been growing, the belief in "givenness" has declined. We who have claimed a Manifest Destiny now find that the destiny seems suddenly to have lost its manifestness. More than ever we feel that we are cast in a great role, but, for the first time, we begin to wonder if we ourselves may not have some responsibility for composing the plot.

We can date this decline in our sense of "givenness" from somewhere around the end of the nineteenth century. It was then that historians began to discover what had distinguished the history of our institutions. The uniqueness of American history was fully discovered only after, and perhaps because, what had given us that uniqueness seemed about to disappear.

The historical skill and poetic imagination of Frederick Jackson Turner then produced an interpretation that was more an autopsy than an anatomy of our institutions. Turner's famous lecture, "The Significance of the Frontier in American History," which he delivered in 1893, was a declaration of the uniqueness of the American past. It was equally a prophecy of a lack of uniqueness in the American future. The critical fact which had made the history of the United States different from that of

Europe was ceasing to exist. Uniqueness would henceforth have to be transmitted through institutions shaped by a unique past, which would enter on a more cosmopolitan future. "And now, four centuries from the discovery of America, at the end of a hundred years of life under the Constitution, the frontier has gone, and with its going has closed the first period of American history." Increasing urbanism, increasing reliance on government, and the growth of large combinations both of capital and of labor were symptoms that America might thenceforth go the way of Europe. "Today," Turner added in 1914, "we are looking with a shock upon a changed world."

The peculiar American experience in dealing with the West was what, according to Turner, had "vitalized all American democracy, and . . . brought it into sharp contrasts with the democracies of history, and with those modern efforts of Europe to create an artificial democratic order by legislation." It would be hard to state the idea more succinctly than he did in a familiar passage:

> American democracy was born of no theorist's dream; it was not carried in the *Sarah Constant* to Virginia, nor in the *Mayflower* to Plymouth. It came out of the American forest, and it gained new strength each time it touched a new frontier. Not the constitution, but free land and abundance of natural resources open to a fit people, made the democratic type of society in America for three centuries while it occupied its empire [*The Frontier in American History* (New York, 1920), p. 293].

The great American political philosopher had been the American land. But now the situation had changed. The uniqueness, and with it the sense of "givenness," was disappearing.

Our Cultural Hypochondria

Our foreign relations were pushing us in the same direction. As we became an actor on the world stage, we were under pressures to defend our institutions before the world. For the first time it appeared that we might have a duty not merely to fulfil our destiny but to describe it.

The spectacle of a professor of political science in the chair of the President of the United States was a symptom of these new tendencies in American life. The phenomenon of President Woodrow Wilson, a man who had some reputation for philosophizing about democracies and governments in general, was something new. And it was something that could hardly have occurred in the United States before the disappearance of the frontier.

Even before the first World War, actually as early as the turn of the century, there were attempts to provide a philosophical substitute for the frontier. Perhaps the most significant, and surely one of the most strenuous, of such efforts was that by Josiah Royce. We have some clue to what was happening to the sense of "givenness" if we compare the flavor of his writing with that of the great American yea-sayers of the early and middle nineteenth century.

Those earlier yea-sayers had, on the whole, found it enough to *affirm*—vigorously, eloquently, paradoxically—without defining too sharply what it was they were affirming. Emerson, for instance, in his plea for refreshment in his "American Scholar" (1837) asked that "the single man plant himself indomitably on his instincts"; he complained that " we are embarrassed with second thoughts." In a word, he asked Americans to be themselves; then they would be the best of men and the purest of Americans. Whitman, too, a few years later, was singing of "oneself" and of the bridges and rivers and cities and fields and everything that surrounded the American. If the American only would not resist the influence of his environment, he would be a man. Carl Sandburg, whose first volume of poems appeared in 1916, was one of the latest of this "givenness" school—and perhaps the last who could so readily find values emerging from the total American experience.

From the notion that "what you don't know won't hurt you," the notion that the common experience was enough, Americans moved to the fear that if they did not discover where they were going, they might find themselves going nowhere at all, or even in the wrong direction. To men like Josiah Royce (who had been raised in California in the era of Henry George) it no longer seemed enough in 1908 to urge men to be themselves or to draw in the essence of the American scene. In his *Philosophy of Loyalty*, speaking in a vocabulary he had learned in Germany, Royce sought, with metaphysical clarity and something like Kantian subtlety, to lay bare community ideals.

Now, it seemed, one had a double problem: first, to define the task; and only then to try to accomplish it. There was a novel and transatlantic sound to Royce's plea to "bring back to the first rank of interest once more the problems of Goethe's *Faust* and of Kant's *Critique*." Royce asked for a clear description of "the true goal of men's actions." "Send us the thinker," he pleaded in his

"Decay of Earnestness" (1881), "that can show us just what in life is most worthy of our toil, just what makes man's destiny more than poor and comic, just what is the ideal that we ought to serve; let such a thinker point out to us plainly that ideal, and then say, in a voice that we must hear, 'Work, work for that; it is the highest'—then such a thinker will have saved our age from one-sidedness, and have given it eternal significance" (*Fugitive Essays* [New York, 1920], p. 303).

The weaknesses of Royce's philosophy were a symbol of the difficulties confronting an American social philosopher. While his philosophy of loyalty provided an absolutist strongbox for American values, when one opened the box, one found it contained almost nothing: he urged his readers to be loyal to the principal of loyalty.

Liberals like Herbert Croly, for example, writing in his *Promise of American Life* in 1909, were bitterly critical of the old "easy, generous, irresponsible optimism." This is the way they characterized the traditional belief that American values were implicit in American institutions. And they looked toward "converting our American national destiny into a national purpose," by which they usually meant the deliberate organization of American society around a well-articulated, comprehensive, and defensible social philosophy. It is significant that this new insistence on philosophical definition came from people like Josiah Royce, Henry George, and Herbert Croly, who, almost without exception, wanted a larger role for the state, a role more like what was familiar in nineteenth-century Europe, where political parties embodied political philosophies.

With each national crisis of the twentieth century the demand for explicitness has recurred. During the last ten years we have heard more and more voices asking for a "democratic faith" or a philosophy for democracy. Many Americans have come to feel that they ought to have a personal philosophy adequate in clarity and subtlety to the new responsibility of every American for the state of the world. It is no less the sense of national power than the sense of personal inadequacy that has driven us to seek clear and outspoken doctrines to guide us. The decline in the sense of "givenness" has made our problem acute.

We have found symptoms of this decline in some turning from the generalized religion described in the last chapter, to a more precise, more theological, and more dogmatic religion. Among Protestants we find a growing interest in attempts, like those of Reinhold Niebuhr, to sharpen and elaborate their theology. Among Catholics, a desire to invigorate their doctrine, an interest in the writings of Jacques Maritain and Yves Simon, and the phenomenon of Thomas Merton. Among Jews, a self-conscious quest for redefinition, exemplified in the success of *Commentary* magazine. We have seen a general movement of many intellectuals toward Catholicism, illustrated by a number of notable conversions. Many of these efforts, including a growing interest in political theory and philosophy in our colleges, are symptoms of the declining sense of "givenness," of the attempt of individuals to attain for themselves, even at great personal cost, the kind of thing which until recently seemed to be given to all Americans gratis.

Is the sense of "givenness," which I have described in this book, about to disappear? Can we preserve it? If not, what can take its place? I can see two, and only two, alternatives.

The first would be to answer the demand for a democratic philosophy directly, by trying to build one. But, as I have tried to show, we are traditionally ill qualified for such an enterprise. Moreover, any such attempt to agree on the tenets of our agreement is liable to be self-defeating. When people already agree, the effort to define what they agree on is more likely to produce conflict than accord. Precise definitions are more often the end than the beginning of agreement.

The second possibility is to try to bring to the surface those attitudes which have been latent in the notion of "givenness" itself, to discover the general truths about institutions by which we have actually lived. If anything can be done to perpetuate the virtues of our political thought, in my opinion it must be along these latter lines. For any such enterprise of self-discovery, Burke provided us a motto in his "Letter to the Sheriffs of Bristol on the Affairs of America" (1777):

> Civil freedom . . . is not, as many have endeavoured to persuade you, a thing that lies hid in the depth of abstruse science. It is a blessing and a benefit, not an abstract speculation; and all the just reasoning that can be upon it is of so coarse a texture, as perfectly to suit the ordinary capacities of those who are to enjoy, and of those who are to defend it . . . social and civil freedom, like all other things in common life, are variously

mixed and modified, enjoyed in very different degrees, and shaped into an infinite diversity of forms, according to the temper and circumstances of every community.

If we choose this alternative, we will be reticent about our ability to displace history by philosophy. We will be humble before our past and the past of other nations; for we will seek the wisdom in institutions.

II. THE "SEAMLESSNESS" OF CULTURE

It is important at this point to prepare ourselves for an anticlimax. When we penetrate the Holy of Holies of our national faith, we must not expect the glittering jewels and filigreed relics of a pagan temple. The story is told that when the Temple of Solomon in Jerusalem fell in 63 B.C. and Pompey invaded the Holy of Holies, he found to his astonishment that it was empty. This was, of course, a symbol of the absence of idolatry, which was the essential truth of Judaism. Perhaps the same surprise awaits the student of American culture, if he finally manages to penetrate the arcanum of our belief. And for a similar reason.

Far from being disappointed, we should be inspired that in an era of idolatry, when so many nations have filled their sanctuaries with ideological idols, we have had the courage to refuse to do so. What I shall try to pass off on you as the content of the *sanctum* ought more precisely to be described as something very different: namely, the tenets which have enabled us to keep the *sanctum* empty.

Before I describe these tenets, I should briefly indicate what I mean by the idolatry from which we have managed to keep ourselves free. It is the idolatry which would put the thorough plan of a particular generation in place of the accumulating wisdom of tradition and institutions. Its twin deities are the Goddess of Reason (worshiped in the French Revolution), and the God of Force and Uniformity (worshiped in more recent European revolutions).

The modern life of this pagan cult can be traced back to the Romantic movement of the eighteenth and early nineteenth centuries. To make *any* headway against the institutional debris which covered the European landscape in those days; to take even short, halting steps toward a democratic, equalitarian society; to allow the freedom and initiative without which modern capitalism would have been inconceivable, it was perhaps necessary to impress on men an exaggerated sense of their power to remake society. Rousseau was, appropriately, the patron saint of Romantic arrogance.

Political dreamers in Europe in the eighteenth and nineteenth centuries *had* to lead a rich fantasy life, precisely because their *real* political life was so frustrating. But America was the land of dreams-come-true; for the oppressed European, life in America was itself fantasy. It was not necessary here to develop a theory to prove that man could begin anew, that decent community was possible; life in America seemed itself sufficient proof. As De Tocqueville remarked:

At no time has the American people laid hold on ideas of this kind [the general ideas of the French Revolution] with the passionate energy of the French people in the eighteenth century, or displayed the same blind confidence in the value and abso-

lute truth of any theory. . . . The Americans are a democratic
people who have always directed public affairs themselves. The
French are a democratic people who for a long time could only
speculate on the best manner of conducting them. The social
condition of the French led them to conceive very general ideas
on the subject of government, while their political constitution
prevented them from correcting those ideas by experiment and
from gradually detecting their insufficiency; whereas in America
the two things constantly balance and correct each other [*Democracy in America*, II, 18].

The American experience was in several ways a check
on romantic vagaries. Not only was there less need felt
for theories in general. But, specifically, the American
was to find reasons of his own to doubt many of the more
simple-minded notions of the Romantics.

It was easy enough for Rousseau or Wordsworth or
Shelley to assert that man could remake himself by making over his institutions. In Europe such an assertion
would be free from risk of disproof, precisely because
such an opportunity could never really exist on that continent. Whenever an attempt at wholesale revolution
failed or bred tyranny, one could charge it to the fact
that the revolution had not been wholesale enough or
that its high purposes had been blighted by a Napoleon,
a Stalin, or a Hitler.

But in America the opportunity *was* real; and men—
even the most optimistic—could observe with their own
eyes the limitations on man's power to remake his institutions. Because we in America, more than other peoples
of modern history, *seemed* situated to start life anew,
we have been better able to see how much man inevitably

retains of his past. For here, even with an unexampled opportunity for cultural rebirth, the American has remained plainly the inheritor of European laws, culture, and institutions.

America has thus been both the laboratory and the nemesis of romanticism. While the American experience would surely dishearten a visionary like Thoreau, it could actually encourage a Puritan or a Jeffersonian. The belief that man could change his institutions at will and that from such changes utopia would flow was perhaps the most basic of the romantic illusions to dissolve in America.

But this was not all. Take the concept of the Noble Savage, the anthropological corollary of the opening words of Rousseau's *Émile*, "God makes all things good; man meddles with them and they become evil." The American could know that a wild, new environment would not cure all the ills of man's nature. It was easy and even witty to praise the savage from a European drawing-room; but Americans who had been the targets of the Indian's arrows and had seen him in his habitat would (except for a rare James Fenimore Cooper) find the idea of the Noble Savage a pretty bad joke. One could provide still other examples of how the American experience itself has been a providential solvent of romantic illusions. Only when men were forced to live out their illusions did they see how illusory they really were.

Nothing could be more absurd than to try to make of the isolated utopian communities in American history anything like a great tradition of utopianism in the main stream of our thought. Some of our historians, desperately searching for articulateness and for ties with the European traditions of socialism, have attempted just this. They miss the essential point that the whole American experience has been utopian.

We have, of course, had our New Harmonys, our Brook Farms, and our Oneidas; but these have been, at most, minor tributaries of our thought. Their most important legacy has probably been a deepened skepticism of all such enterprises. As Hawthorne observes in his Preface to *The Blithedale Romance* (a novel about Brook Farm), that community was a kind of American version of "Faery Land."

The one conspicuously successful movement in American history which has had a utopian character has been the Mormon church. We need not here ask how much its doctrinal compromises have had to do with its survival. But in accounting for the remarkable success of Mormonism, we must remember that Mormon theology supplements the Old and the New Testaments with a gospel which declares the Promised Land to be America.

In trying to explain how we have managed to keep our sanctum empty of idols, I cannot, of course, offer any rounded political philosophy, for that is precisely what we have not had. But it may be possible to describe an attitude—a kind of principle implicit in the idea of "givenness"—which has enabled us to avoid idolatry. I am afraid the principle is extremely prosaic, but that does not make it any less true. Actually, it is the converse of what some cultivated European critics have called an American weakness: namely, our ineptness at making distinctions. Whether or not this be a philosophic weakness, its opposite is surely a virtue, namely, our tendency to see things as wholes. This might be called a sense for the "seamlessness" of experience. Aspects of experience which are elsewhere sharply distinguished here seem to merge into each other: the private and the public, the religious and the political, even—as I have suggested—the "is" and the "ought," the world of fact and the world of fancy, of science and of morals.

The principle of the "seamlessness" of experience has two elements. This sense of wholeness, the feeling for the continuum of experience, is expressed in relation both to space and to time.

1. First it is a way of describing the organic nature of society. This is the sense of seamlessness of experience in *space:* that institutions, and especially political institutions, are intimately related to the peculiar environment which nourishes them. It comes from sensitivity to the fact that American values arise out of a frontier, that the politics and culture of the city are one thing, those of the country another; that the problems of America may be of one kind, those of Europe of another.

This is a generalized version of our idea of "givenness": the idea that the values and form of institutions are shaped and ought to be shaped by the landscape in which they grow. As Stephen Vincent Benét wrote in the opening lines of *John Brown's Body:*

> American muse, whose strong and diverse heart
> So many men have tried to understand
> But only made it smaller with their art,
> Because you are as various as your land. . . .

The notion is pragmatic: good political institutions are those which enable a people to seize their unique opportunities. It is conservative: it presupposes a certain national character or destiny as always in a sense given, given by the circumstances of geography and history. Its corollary is a suspicion of grand schemes which seek to make over the character of men or institutions. American experience has engraved in our consciousness the idea of culture as a matrix; *our* politics, religion, economy, and ideas all seem so obviously related to the special conditions of life in America that we have had forced on us the connection of *all* institutions with their context.

Thus it is much harder to understand many institutions and ideas here than in countries where the aspects of experience are more sharply distinguished. As I have suggested, the boundaries of religion and politics are vaguer here than elsewhere. Or take our concept of equality, which many have called the central American value. No sooner does one describe a subject like this and try to separate it for study, than one finds it diffusing and evaporating into the general atmosphere. "Equality," what does it mean? In the United States it has been taken for a fact and an ideal, a moral imperative and a sociological datum, a legal principle and a social norm. It describes a continuum from physiology at one end to theology at the other.

The very concept of federalism is based on the principle of the "seamlessness" of culture: it assumes the necessity of allowing much autonomy to each region. It arises from awareness that regions are different and that different regions must have somewhat different institutions. Thus our federalism actually implies an organic approach to society, the realization that institutions always grow out-of-doors in a particular climate and cannot be carried about in a flower pot.

2. The second aspect of the principle of "seamlessness" asserts the historical continuity of institutions. This is the counterpart in *time*, of the organic concept in space. As we have seen, even the great crises in our history—the Revolution and the Civil War—have expressed and affirmed this continuity. I have already referred to the old saw that the European has a sense of relation to the past, while the American is set down, as it were, without foundations. But that view is superficial, based on the calendar rather than on the meaning of the past to living people.

For, as I have suggested, much of what the European sees of the past—especially today—emphasizes his separation from it. His past is longer, but at least his recent past is far more motley and discontinuous than ours. Many crucial events of recent European history have been attempts at historical amnesia: each successive epoch denies that the preceding age expressed its true self or sometimes even refuses to admit that the earlier age existed.

The French Revolution of the eighteenth century, in its radical phase, was a strenuous denial of the past; French history in the nineteenth century was an alternation of violently republican and violently monarchical spirits; even today there the basic opposition of political parties is among groups which stand for radically different images of the national history. In Germany, especially during the last century, the oscillations have been more violent and much more costly both to that country and to mankind; the Nazis stood for the German Volk and seemed so to the majority of Germans for at least a decade; they made an effort to forget or even deny 1848; now, of course, the "denial" of the Nazi past is equally enthusiastic. Even in Great Britain, the fall of the British Empire and the coming of socialism have dug a gulf between past and present.

How different is our American relation to our past! If our past has been more brief, we feel much closer to it than do the peoples of Europe. As I pointed out in the first chapter, most of what we see of our past reinforces our feeling of continuity and oneness with it. In a certain sense, of course, the Civil War dug a gulf in our history; but it is a gulf which, for different reasons, both northerners and southerners have been eager to deny. We have seen how North and South each considered the war its own way of affirming the single true American past; and the matter has remained discussable, not in revolutionary, but in legal, language.

Our periods of national glory and power have not been periods of explicit denial of the preceding stages. Washington and Jefferson and Adams and Jackson and Lincoln have seemed the contemporaries of all their great successors. This would even be true of the New Deal. According to the orthodox Republican interpretation, many of Franklin D. Roosevelt's measures (at least the more successful ones) were actually initiated by Herbert Hoover.

The American who goes to Europe cannot but be shocked by the casualness with which Frenchmen or Italians view the possibility of violent change in their society. Of course, if this had not been so, life might have been unbearable for them during the last century. The unspoken question lies beneath all their personal decisions: What might be the consequences of this or that course of action if society should suddenly become Communist or Fascist, or whatnot? For the European the past, and therefore the future, seems a kind of grab bag of extreme alternatives. Because for us the past is a solid stalk out of which our present seems to grow, the lines of our future seem clearer and more inevitable.

It is not surprising that we have no enthusiasm for plans to make society over. We have actually made a new society without a plan. Or, more precisely, why should *we* make a five-year plan for ourselves when God seems to have had a thousand-year plan ready-made for us?

Our history inclines us, then, to see fascism and naziism and communism not merely as bad philosophies but as violations of the essential nature of institutions. To us institutions have appeared as a natural continuum with the non-institutional environment and the historical past. From this point of view, the proper role of the citizen and the statesman here is one of conservation and reform rather than of invention. He is free to occupy himself with the means of improving his society; for there is relatively little disagreement on ends. Turner summed it up when he said: "The problem of the United States is not to create democracy, but to conserve democratic institutions and ideals."

Nothing could be more mistaken than to assume that such an approach need be smug, uncritical, or unprogressive. On the contrary, no one is more smug than the crusader. If you have ever talked to a thorough Communist or Fascist, you know what I mean. The True Believer always seems to think that his mere possession of his golden nuggets is an overwhelming virtue. "My strength is as the strength of ten, because my heart is pure." Few would want Sir Galahad for president of the United States, but many peoples of Europe seem to yearn for such leadership. One of the grimmest caricatures of this yearning was the picture postal card, widely disseminated in Nazi Germany, of Adolf Hitler wearing the armor of a knight, mounted on a white charger, in the role of Siegfried. On the other hand, the man with his eye on institutions can never fail to recognize his own inadequacy. He sees the complexity of his task and the constant need for improvement. He can never rest in the puffing satisfaction of righteous knowledge.

If what I have said is correct, the accidents of the American past fit us not only for a skepticism of doctrinaire politics but also for a lively sense of tradition. As T. S. Eliot has said, tradition depends on the historical sense, and "the historical sense involves a perception, not only of the pastness of the past, but of its presence."

Through no special virtue or effort of our own, we may be peculiarly fitted for the role which we are called on to play. But our attitude to institutions can survive only so long as we preserve our sense for the uniqueness of the American experience. A wholesome conservatism rests on knowledge of what is peculiarly valuable in the things to be conserved. The science of uniqueness is the study of history, and our feeling for the uniqueness of our culture will be proportionate to our knowledge of our past.

III. THE GENIUS OF AMERICAN POLITICS

The doom which awaited the Roman Empire, according to C. N. Cochrane, "was that of a civilization which failed to understand itself and was, in consequence, dominated by a haunting fear of the unknown." Much the same could be said for us. Our intellectual insecurity, our feeling of philosophical inadequacy, may be explained at least in part by our failure to understand ourselves. This failure is due in some measure to our readiness to accept the European clichés about us.

We all know that people are prone to parade their weaknesses as if they were virtues. Anyone who has recently been among Europeans can tell you that there is an increasing tendency on the old continent to blame the United States for lacking many of the ills which have characterized European history. Our lack of poverty is called materialism, our lack of political dogma is called aimlessness and confusion. On the whole, the people, and especially the intellectuals of Europe, who are desperately on the offensive, have succeeded in convincing us—and especially our intellectuals. They have made us apologize for our wealth and welfare. You will find many well-meaning Americans abroad who think that they are defending their country when they point out that people in the United States are really a lot worse off than Europeans think. They have made us apologize for our lack of philosophical clarity, so that we seek to concoct a political philosophy which can rival the dogmas of Europe.

It has been too long since we have stood on the special virtues of our life and our continent. Over a century has passed since Emerson declared in his "American Scholar": "Our day of dependence, our long apprenticeship to the learning of other lands, draws to a close. The millions that around us are rushing into life, cannot always be fed on the sere remains of foreign harvests." But we still see ourselves in the distorting mirror of Europe.

The image which Europe shows us is as much a defense of itself as a caricature of us. We are too easily persuaded that the cancers of European life (and especially of European political life) are healthy growths and that we are deformed for not possessing them. The equations of poverty and idealism, of monopoly and responsibility, of aristocracy and culture, of political dogma and purposeful political institutions, are too readily accepted. It is, of course, some solace to a declining European culture —a culture dying of poverty, monopoly, aristocracy, and ideology—to think that their ills are simply the excess of their virtues. That theirs must be the virtues of all cultures. And hence that the accidents of history which may have immunized us against such vices also sterilize our culture and doom us to philistinism and vagrancy.

Our Cultural Hypochondria

There is no denying that our intellectuals and, most of all, our academics, being the most cosmopolitan part of our culture, have been especially susceptible to the well-meaning advice of our sick friends in Europe. Like many sick friends, they are none too sorry to be able to tell us that *we* are not in the best of health.

We have, in a word, been too easily led to deny our peculiarly American virtues, in order to seem to have the peculiar European vices. Moreover, our intellectuals, who rightly consider themselves the critical organ of our community, have been much too sensitive to any charge of chauvinism. Hence they, too, have been readier to tell us what we lack than to help us discover what we have. Our historians and political scientists, while blaming themselves and one another for "irresponsibility," have failed to help us discover the peculiar virtues of our situation. They have left the discovery and defense of those virtues to the dubious efforts of professional patriots.

Is it any wonder that the very word "patriotism" should come to be suspect among intellectuals? Is it any wonder that we suffer from cultural hypochondria?

The cure for our hypochondria is surely not chauvinism. That simply adds one real ill to the many unreal ills of which we already accuse ourselves. Waving a flag cannot cure inner uncertainty. One possibility, at least a little more fruitful, is to try to discover the peculiar virtues of our situation, the special character of our history: to try to judge ourselves by the potentialities of our own peculiar and magnificent continent. We may then discover that our virtues, like our ills, are actually peculiar to ourselves; that what seem to be inadequacies of our culture, if measured by European standards, are nothing but our differences and may even be virtues.

We are sure to lose the intellectual struggle if we accept the terms of the debate as posed by Russia and by Europe; if we try to show that we are a new and more perfect embodiment of the European ideal of political institutions and culture. That we certainly are not. The European concept of a political community is of a group oriented toward fulfilling an explicit philosophy; political life there is the world of ends and absolutes.

The European concept of culture is basically aristocratic; its great successes—especially in countries like Italy and France—are in the aristocratic arts. Its literature is for the few; its newspapers are subsidized by political parties; its books, when successful, have a circulation a fifth of that in America, even in proportion to the population. European culture, most of it at least, is the heritage of a pre-liberal past. For all their magnificence, the monuments of that past are products of a culture with which we, fortunately, are in no position to compete. It is surely no accident that we have accomplished relatively little in the arts of painting, sculpture, palace and church architecture, chamber music, and chamber poetry. It is equally no accident that we have contributed so little in political philosophy.

Some Americans, however—and they are probably increasing in number—make the un-American demand for a philosophy of democracy. They believe that this philosophy will be a weapon against Russia and a prop for our own institutions. They are afraid that, without some such salable commodity, they may not be able to compete with Russia in the world market.

These people are puzzled that we should have come as far as we have without knowing the philosophy which lies beneath our institutions. They are even frightened at what they might find—or fail to find—when they open the *sanctum sanctorum* of national belief. It is these who are among our most dangerous friends; for, even if they should find the Holy of Holies empty, they would refuse to admit it. Instead of trying to discover the reasons why we have managed to be free of idolatry, they will make their own graven image, their own ass's head, and say that is what belonged in the temple all the time. These people are dangerous because they would misrepresent us abroad and corrupt us at home.

If we have no exportable political theory, then can we export our political institutions? Should we try to induce the Italian or the German people to become democratic in the American image? If the thesis of this book is correct, the answer here too is, of course, No. The answer is No, not merely because the attempt to distil our philosophy or to transplant our institutions is apt to fail. It is No, because the principles on which we approach politics and have succeeded in building our own institutions, deny such a possibility.

If we have learned anything from our history, it is the wisdom of allowing institutions to develop according to the needs of each particular environment; and the value of both environmentalism and traditionalism as principles of political life, as ways of saving ourselves from the imbecilities, the vagaries, and the cosmic enthusiasms of individual men. This is our idea of constitutional federalism, without which our great union would have been impossible.

If what has held us together as a nation has been no explicit political theory held in common but rather a fact of life (what Whitman properly called "adhesiveness"), how can we expect to bind other nations by theories? We have felt both "individualism which isolates" and, as he says, "adhesiveness or love, that fuses, ties, and aggregates."

We have traditionally held out to the world, not our doctrine, but our example. The idea of America as the last best hope of mankind has not been the idea that America would outdo other ages and places with its philosophy. It was life, and not thought, which would excel here. This has perhaps taken some of the sting of arrogance out of our consciousness of destiny. For men are in the habit of claiming more personal credit for the quality of their thought than for the quality of their institutions. Even to the most obtuse, institutions seem the product of many forces. In the past we have wanted to be judged not by what we could *tell* the world but by what we could *show* the world. Moreover, we have considered ourselves not a factory of institutions but a laboratory, an experiment. By showing what man might do under our new circumstances, we might give men everywhere new hope for improving their lot *after their own fashion.*

No one has stated the case better than did John C. Calhoun, speaking at the time of the Mexican War, about a century ago:

It has been lately urged in a very respectable quarter, that it is the mission of this country to spread civil and religious liberty over all the globe, and especially over this continent—even by force, if necessary. It is a sad delusion. . . . It is a remarkable fact in the political history of man, that there is scarcely an instance of a free constitutional government, which has been the work exclusively of foresight and wisdom. They have all been the result of a fortunate combination of circumstances [*Works*, IV, 416].

It is our experience, not our dogma or our power, that may be the encouragement and the hope of the world. We can, Calhoun concluded, "do more to extend liberty by our example over this country and the world generally, than would be done by a thousand victories."

To tell people what institutions they must have, whether we tell them with the Voice of America or with the Money of America, is the thorough denial of our American heritage. It would be an attempt "to meet the monolithic East by attempting to set up a monolithic West." As Stephen Spender has observed, "When the Communists today congratulate themselves on being 'monolithic,' they are congratulating themselves on being dead: and it is for us to see that they do not turn the whole world into their cemetery." An imposed democracy expresses a corroding cynicism. And democratic institutions, however much they may rest on pessimism, must be the opposite of cynical. Tyrannies—fascism, naziism, communism—can impose themselves on others with no hypocrisy, for they rest unashamedly on force. But if we were to become cynical in order to make Europe *seem* to stand for something better than it might on its own, we would risk losing everything, even if we should win.

Is it not even possible that the people of Europe will be more willing to defend themselves if it is their own institutions they are defending? If they are unwilling to defend their own, they surely will not want to defend ours.

We have, of course, our modern abolitionists, those who believe that the abolition of slavery in Russia is the sole issue in the world. They surely need no philosophy. The clarity and righteousness of their objective is enough. Soviet communism provides them the sense of "givenness," of obviousness in their objective. For them, Communists embody the spirit of Satan as vividly as the American Indians did for the first Puritans, or as the southern slaveowners did for fire-eaters like Phillips and Garrison. Some of them would seem almost as willing as Garrison to burn the Constitution in order to attain their admirable objective.

There are others who take a more practical Lincolnian view. Like Lincoln, these people hate slavery anywhere, but they doubt their capacity to make a perfect world. Their main concern is to preserve and improve free institutions where they now exist.

If the Lincolnian view involves us in the seeming contradiction of defending our institutions without insisting on propagating them, this is nothing but the contradiction within the idea of freedom itself, which affirms a value but asserts it only to allow a competition among values. We must refuse to become crusaders for liberalism, in order to remain liberals. We must refuse to try to export our commodity. We must refuse to become crusaders for conservatism, in order to conserve the institutions and the genius which have made America great.

SUGGESTIONS FOR FURTHER READING

Every student of American culture should read Alexis de
Tocqueville's *Democracy in America* (2 vols.), first published
in English in 1835 and now available in many reprint editions. To
its many insights I am deeply indebted. Herbert Agar's *Price of
Union* (Boston, 1950) gives us a subtle and persuasive analysis of
the American party system, showing in detail how personalities,
economic conditions, and a host of other circumstances have
produced our characteristic system of compromises. Much of the
appeal of V. L. Parrington's *Main Currents in American
Thought* (3 vols.; New York, 1927–30), which has become a classic of our intellectual history, is due to the deftness and dramatic
skill with which he recounts the genesis of American culture as
the development "of certain germinal ideas that have come to be
reckoned traditionally American."

CHAPTER II. THE PURITANS: FROM PROVIDENCE TO PRIDE

The reader first coming to the Puritans has the advantage of
an admirable anthology: Perry Miller and Thomas H. Johnson,
The Puritans (New York, 1938). In addition to selections from
the leading American Pilgrims and Puritans, the volume contains
an excellent critical Bibliography. They, unlike Americans of
some other periods, have left us accounts of their own age which
rank with the best historical works: William Bradford's *History
of Plymouth Plantation,* John Winthrop's *Journal* (sometimes
called *The History of New England*), and Cotton Mather's
Magnalia Christi Americana. All these have been several times
reprinted.

CHAPTER III. THE AMERICAN REVOLUTION: REVOLUTION
WITHOUT DOGMA

The traditional image of the Revolution appears, if sometimes
with the sharpness of caricature, in George Bancroft's *History*

of the United States (especially in Vol. I, Introduction and chap. xix; Vol. IV, chap. xxviii; and Vol. VI, chap. i). There is no better access to the flavor of the political thinking of that age, to the subordination of ideological to practical problems, and to the importance of constitutionalism, than through the pages of *The Federalist,* by Alexander Hamilton, James Madison, and John Jay (many times reprinted). The student who has the stamina and wishes a more extensive and more intimate view of the thinking of the age should not fail to examine the magnificent edition of *The Papers of Thomas Jefferson* (edited by Julian Boyd and published by the Princeton University Press), the successive volumes of which are currently appearing. In my *Lost World of Thomas Jefferson* (New York, 1948), I have tried to describe the spirit of Jeffersonian thought, to see the relation among their different ideas, and to define the characteristically American flavor of their world-view. Suggestive discussion, from different points of view, of the problem of conservatism and the Revolution is found in: Merrill Jensen, *The New Nation, 1781–1789* (New York, 1950), and Leonard W. Labaree, *Conservatism in Early American History* (New York, 1948). Louis Hartz's brilliant article, "American Political Thought and the American Revolution," *American Political Science Review,* XLVI (1952), 321–42, which did not come to my attention until after this chapter had gone to press, arrives at a conclusion not far from mine, although by a rather different route. Of the many general interpretive essays on the era, I especially recommend Carl Becker's *Declaration of Independence* (New York, 1922), C. H. McIlwain's *American Revolution* (New York, 1923), and Randolph G. Adams, *Political Ideas of the American Revolution* (Durham, N.C., 1922). Alexis de Tocqueville's *Ancien Régime,* a brilliant study of the background of the French Revolution of 1789, remains a suggestive foil for the study of our Revolution. It is available in a new English translation by M. W. Patterson (Oxford, 1952).

CHAPTER IV. THE CIVIL WAR AND THE SPIRIT OF COMPROMISE

For a perspective on the Civil War, some of the most valuable works are those on the southern side, which have been too com-

Suggestions for Further Reading

monly treated as mere curiosae: especially Alexander Stephens, *A Constitutional View of the Late War between the States* (2 vols.; Philadelphia, 1868–70), and Jefferson Davis, *The Rise and Fall of the Confederate Government* (2 vols.; New York, 1881). For a proper understanding of the constitutional issues, the Constitution of the Confederate States of America (available in many collections of documents) should be read and compared with the federal Constitution. The works of John C. Calhoun, and especially his "Disquisition on Government," are beginning to receive the respect which they deserve; his "Discourse on the Constitution and Government of the United States" should be studied in connection with the "Disquisition." Both are found in Volume I of his *Works,* ed. Richard K. Cralle (6 vols.; New York, 1888). I know of no adequate survey of the "sociological" literature of the pre–Civil War era. For the focusing of interest on this subject, we are indebted to the perceptive studies of Harvey Wish, especially his *George Fitzhugh* (Baton Rouge, La., 1943). Fitzhugh's *Sociology for the South* is a work of much more than topical significance. A handy selection of the writings of Lincoln is the one by Philip Van Doren Stern (New York, 1940). Of the vast Lincoln literature, the recent essays which I have found most helpful and to which I am most indebted are Richard Hofstadter, *The American Political Tradition and the Men Who Made It* (New York, 1948), chap. v; and J. G. Randall, *Lincoln the Liberal Statesman* (New York, 1947).

CHAPTER V. THE MINGLING OF POLITICAL AND RELIGIOUS THOUGHT

While there are a number of excellent studies of the history of particular sects, I know of no adequate sociology of recent American religion. William James's *Varieties of Religious Experience* (New York, 1902) is a classic; apart from its many other virtues, it states eloquently a number of characteristically American assumptions about religion. To the same general effect, though less eloquent, is John Dewey's *A Common Faith* (New Haven, 1934). A valuable study of the mingling of political and religious thought in one period in American history is Alice M. Baldwin, *The New England Clergy and the American*

Revolution (Durham, N.C., 1928). On the relation of popular education to "uplift," Dixon Wector has given us a suggestive essay in *Literary History of the United States,* ed. Robert E. Spiller and others (3 vols.; New York, 1948), II, 798 ff. Walter Lippmann's *Preface to Morals* (New York, 1929) is a sophisticated and sometimes wise statement of what, in one period at least, was taken by intellectuals to be the foundation of their non-denominationalism.

CHAPTER VI. OUR CULTURAL HYPOCHONDRIA AND HOW TO CURE IT

Ralph Waldo Emerson's "American Scholar" (1837) still speaks to us. One can secure some insights into the quest for absolutes in American life through such diverse works as Josiah Royce's *Philosophy of Loyalty* (New York, 1908); Herbert Croly's *Promise of American Life* (New York, 1909); R. H. Crossman (ed.), *The God That Failed* (New York, 1950), especially the chapters by Richard Wright and Louis Fischer; and Whittaker Chambers' *Witness* (New York, 1952). A sound statement of the relation of the constitutional tradition to recent American problems is found in C. H. McIlwain's *Constitutionalism Ancient and Modern* (Ithaca, N.Y., 1940).

INDEX

Index

Ingersoll, Robert G., 156
Instrumentalism, 141–42; *see also* Religion
Intellectuals, 181, 183
"Irrepressible Conflict," 112

Jackson, Andrew, 29
James, William, 141, 143–44, 152
Jameson, J. Franklin, 69
Jay, John, 96, 97
Jefferson, Thomas: and American Revolution, 84–94; and anthropology, 71; Carl Becker on, 78; Colonial period, 86; cosmopolitan period, 86; on extent of republic, 102; as lawyer, 87; and legal reform, 91–94; and mottoes, 92; and nationalism, 73; as political philosopher, 66; and political theory, 85–86; as preacher, 159; on slavery, 114; *Summary View*, 89; and Virginia Constitution, 89
Jeffersonians, 17
Jensen, Merrill, 69
Jews, 141, 168
John Brown's Body, 175
Johnson, Edward, 56
Jonathan, 7
Journey in the Back Country, 117
Judaism, 141, 147, 170

King Philip's War, 54

Leaves of Grass, 159
"Letter to the Sheriffs of Bristol on the Affairs of America," 169–70
Leverett, John, 55
Lewis, Sinclair, 20
Lincoln, Abraham: and Blackstone, 88; on compromise, 130–31; Gettysburg Address, 12; as national hero, 29; as orator, 155; and political theory, 20; as preacher, 159; religion of, 136, 145; and Revolutionary tradi-

tion, 126; on slavery, 113–14; and slavery today, 188; on Union, 131
Locke, John, 2, 78, 97
Long, Huey, 156
Loyalty oaths, 153

McIlwain, Charles H., 76
Madison, James, 11, 96, 97, 101–2
Magna Charta, 15, 18, 94
Magnalia Christi Americana, 57–60
Manifest destiny, 163
Maritain, Jacques, 168
Marshall, John, 87
Marx, Karl, 3, 76
Mason, George, 91
Mather, Cotton, 55, 57–60
Mather, Increase, 48, 55
Mencken, H. L., 20, 147
Merton, Thomas, 168
Michelangelo, 29
Mickey Mouse, 32
Mill, J. S., 97
Miller, Arthur, 29
Montesquieu, Baron de, 101
Morgan, Lewis H., 104
Mormons, 174
Morton, Charles, 55
Mother's Day, 146, 154
Mottoes, 92
Mussolini, 13

Napoleon, 29, 172
National Conference of Christians and Jews, 146
Natural history, 55
Naziism, 3, 7, 65, 178, 179
Negro, and Civil War, 111–14
New Deal, 178
New Harmony, 174
Newton, Sir Isaac, 78
Niebuhr, Reinhold, 152, 168
Noble Savage, 173
Non-denominationalism, 139, 145–49; *see also* Religion
North, Lord, 72
Norton, John, 40, 46
Notes on Virginia, 114

Index

Oaths, 153
Olmsted, Frederick L., 116–17
Oneida, 174
Oratory, 149–50, 155–57
Orthodoxy, 13–14, 124–32, 138–40
Otis, James, 72

Paine, Thomas, 74
Palmer raids, 14
Paul, 9
Pendleton, Edmund, 86, 91
Pessimism, 187–88
Phillips, Wendell, 111, 112, 188
Philosophy of Loyalty, 166
Pilgrims, 10, 41–42
Plato, 2, 97
Political parties, 17, 137–40
Political theory: defined, 2; and education, 159–60; and religion, 133–60; and sociology, 101–18
Political thought; *see* "Givenness"; Political theory
Pompey, 170
Poor Richard, 159
Preachers, 159
"Preformation": and Civil War debate, 130; and constitution, 15; defined, 10; and experimentation, 20
Private life, 158
Promise of American Life, 167
Propaganda, 4, 160, 186–87
Protestants, 141, 168
Providence, 46–47, 49
Puritans, 36–65; on America, 24; American distinguished, 39; and American Revolution, 13; and church membership, 61–63; decline of, 38, 51–63; and Devil, 43–45; and Halfway Covenant, 61–63; and historical writing, 56–60; and holidays, 60–61; and pride, 39; purpose of, 13; and wilderness, 40–51

Quakers, 157

Raynal, Abbé, 71
Reader's Digest, 154
Religion: and best sellers, 152; church membership, 135; instrumental character of, 141–42; non-denominationalism, 145–49; personal character of, 143–45; and political thought, 133–60; and sects, 144–45
Republican party, 17
Revolution, American; *see* American Revolution
Rise of American Civilization, 119
Roosevelt, Franklin D.: and New Deal, 178; as orator, 155; and political theory, 20; as preacher, 159
Roosevelt, Theodore, 159
Roman Empire, 13, 31, 146, 181
Romanticism, 132, 173
Rousseau, Jean Jacques, 2, 3, 97, 171–73
Royal Society, 55
Royce, Josiah, 165, 166–67

Sabbath, 141
Sandburg, Carl, 166
"Seamlessness" of culture, 170–81
Sectarianism, 144–45; *see also* Non-denominationalism; Religion
Sectionalism, and Civil War, 100–118
Service clubs, 154
Seward, William H., 112–13
Shelley, Percy Bysshe, 172
Shepard, Thomas, 40
Simon, Yves, 168
Slavery, 104, 107–18
Smith, Alfred E., 148–49
Sociology, and Civil War, 101–18
Sociology for the South, 108–10
Spencer, Herbert, 104
Spender, Stephen, 187
"Spread-eagle style," 149

199

PHOENIX BOOKS

in Political Science

PHOENIX BOOKS
in Law

PHOENIX BOOKS
in History

PHOENIX BOOKS
in Business and Economics

PHOENIX BOOKS
in Religion

PHOENIX BOOKS
in Philosophy

PHOENIX BOOKS

in Sociology

PHOENIX BOOKS
Literature and Language

PHOENIX BOOKS
in Art, Music, Poetry, and Drama

PHOENIX POETS